50d

WITHDRAWN

D0907680

The Complete Guide to Self-

Publishing

Copyright © Ben Galley 2014

The right of Ben Galley to be identified as the author and publisher of this work has been asserted in accordance with the Copyright, Designs and Patents Act 1988. All rights reserved.

No part of this book may be used, edited, transmitted in any form or by any means (electronic, mechanical, photocopying, recording or otherwise), or reproduced in any manner without permission except in the case of brief quotations embodied in reviews or articles. It may not be lent, resold, hired out or otherwise circulated without the publisher's permission.

Permission can be obtained through www.bengalley.com

The Shelf Help brand and logo are the property of Ben Galley, as is the 'Polish Publish, Promote' structure.

Limit of Liability/Disclaimer of Warranty: While those responsible for producing this book have used their best efforts in preparing the information contained within the book, they make no representations or warranties with respect to the accuracy or completeness of the contents of this book. The advice and methods explained by the author are the result of extensive experience and research, and although many alternative options are outlined within the text, it is possible that some advice may not be suitable for your particular situation. The author shall not be held liable for any loss of profit or any other commercial damages.

SHCGPB1
978-0-9927871-1-0
1st edition 2014 – Paperback
Published by BenGalley.com
Cover design by Kit Foster
Edited by Poble Sec Books
Illustrations by Hannah New

i

To all my fellow authors out there, who share the passion only a writer can know so well.

This book is for you.

About Ben Galley

Ben Galley is a young self-published author from sunny England and the author of the epic and gritty fantasy series, 'The Emaneska Series'. Ben is incredibly zealous about inspiring other authors and writers. He runs the popular advice site **Shelf Help**, where he offers advice about writing, publishing, and marketing. Ben is also the proud co-founder and director of eBook store **Libiro**, a store exclusive to indie authors. If you want to know more about Ben, he can be found being loquacious and attempting to be witty on Twitter (@BenGalley) or at **www.bengalley.com**.

Contents

Introducing Shelf Help

- Hello   11
- A little introduction   15
- The purpose of this handy guide   19
- A quick note on: self-publishing - a misnomer   20
- The three pillars of Shelf Help self-publishing   22
  - Affordability   23
  - Professionalism   23
  - Technology   23
- How this guide is structured   24

The Industry

- A history of publishing   29
- The Digital Revolution and the rise of self-publishing   33
  - Stigma   35
  - Every ecosystem has its predators   36
- Stats and graphics   39
- So in summary…   43

Part 1: Polish It

- Why your manuscript simply won't do   47
- Editing   49

- Why you need to edit your book 49
  - Ways of editing your book 52
  - Freelance editors 55
    - The different types of editing 56
    - How to find the right editor 57
    - Approaching an editor 58
    - The cost of a pro 59
    - How to work with your editor 61
  - Beta readers 62
    - How to find your beta readers 65
      - Amazon and Goodreads 66
      - Professionals 67
      - Fans 67
      - A quick note on: friends and family 67
    - But how many beta readers will I need? 68
    - Rounding up your betas 69
- Cover design 73
  - Toothpaste 73
  - Deciding what you want on your book cover 75
  - Deciding which format of cover you want 76
  - How to write a blurb 77
  - Sourcing a book cover 78
    - DIY 78
    - Beg, borrow, and steal. Then steal some more. 79
    - Google and recommendations 80
    - Crowd-sourcing 80
    - How much should I be paying for my book cover? 81
    - How do I make sure I get what I pay for? 82
- Formatting 83
  - What is formatting and why do we need to do it? 83
  - The extra bits: 86
    - The copyright page 86
    - The title page 88
    - The 'About the author' page 88

- The table of contents   89
- A quick note on: eBooks and ToCs   89
- The dedication   90
- The acknowledgements   91
- The extra, extra bits   91
- Print formatting   92
- eBook formatting   95
- So in summary…   99

Part 2: Publish It

- What to think about before you think about publishing   105
  - ISBNs   106
  - Metadata   108
  - Prices   110
- Print publishing   113
  - The journey from the printing press to readers' hands   113
    - The traditional model   114
    - The indie model: POD   115
    - The indie model: Bulk printing   116
    - Unit costs, RRPs and wholesale discounts   117
    - A quick note on: making changes   119
  - POD printing   120
    - Lightning Source   120
    - CreateSpace   123
  - Bulk printing   126
    - How to find a bulk printer   128
  - So in summary…   131
- Digital publishing   137
  - Direct eBook publishing Vs eBook distribution   138
    - The direct eBook publishing model   138
    - The eBook distribution model   139
    - A quick note on: consistency and exclusivity   141

- Direct eBook publishing   142
  - KDP and KWL   143
  - A quick note on: DRM, categories and keywords 147
- eBook distribution   149
  - Smashwords Vs BookBaby   150
- So in summary…   152

Part 3: Promote It

- Selling that book of yours   157
- An introduction to marketing   161
- Organic and active marketing   165
- The funnel   169
- Knowledge is power   175
- The Five Golden Rules of marketing   179
- Be Googleable   181
- A quick note on: domain names, hosting and emails 185
- The importance of being social   187
  - My top five platforms?   192
  - How to get started on social media   193
- Getting reviewed   195
  - The four types of reviews   198
    - The starred review   198
    - The media review   199
    - The POS review   199
    - The cover review   200
  - A quick note on: sock-puppetry and paid reviews 201
- Going digital   203
- Content aplenty   207
- Using emails   213
- Let's get physical   215
  - A quick note on: digital data in a physical world 216
  - Local and national press   217

- Merchandise   219
- Posters and flyers   221
- Signings and events   223
- Signings   223
  - How to go about organising a signing   224
  - Getting into indie bookshops and bookshop chains   224
  - Successful signings   226
- Events   227
- Paying your way   229
  - Pay per click   230
  - Pay per impression   232
  - Adverts in magazines and on websites   233
  - Facebook and Twitter ads   234
  - Adverts on radio, TV and public transport   236
  - Marketing agencies   236
- Pricing, giveaways and competitions   239
  - Pricing   239
  - Giveaways and 'perma-free'   240
  - Competitions   241
- So in summary…   242
- My tips for the future   249

Q&As

- Standing on the shoulders of giants   251
- Hugh Howey   253
- Polly Courtney   259
- Joanna Penn   265

A final thank-you   271
Some helpful links   273
A handy glossary   277

Introducing Shelf Help

....

Hello

You are about to undertake an exciting journey.

It was a blustery and bitingly cold Saturday in late 2011. I was seated behind a dwindling pile of my freshly published debut, *The Written*, an epic fantasy novel several years in the forging. It was late afternoon. Shoppers flitted past the bookshop window, hurrying to get back to their warm homes and to something hot and steaming in a mug. I was just starting to consider packing up and calling it a day, and a successful one at that. Plenty of books had been signed and sold, but now the bookshop was winding down to a close, and I was starting to feel the effects of sitting in the same chair for six hours.

But before I could get to my feet and at last stretch my anaesthetised legs, a middle-aged woman, all wrapped up in a bright orange scarf, approached my signing table. She wore an inquisitive expression.

'I've also written a book,' she said.

You could see just the slightest hint of pride in her polite and friendly smile.

I told her that was great and naturally congratulated her. After listening to a brief synopsis of her book (it was a historical romance novel as it turned out, and with every word that smile of hers broadened), I asked her whether she had any plans to publish it. She replied that she did. In fact, she had already started to look for an agent. The woman, who later introduced herself as Gillian, then asked me who my publisher was. I smiled, perhaps betraying some pride of my own, and replied that I was actually self-published. Gillian nodded, quietly said 'I see' and looked around at the bookshop for a moment as if to check that yes, she was indeed in a bookshop. It was then that she asked me a pivotal question.

'So why did you self-publish?' she asked me. The inquisitive look had returned.

As I paused to think of an answer, it abruptly dawned on me: the reason I was sitting in that chair, in that bookshop, on that blustery day.

'Because I can,' I replied.

Gillian answered with a slow nod. Mine was not an answer of arrogance. It stemmed from the realisation of a simple fact: that self-publishing is not a last resort or a consolation prize; it is a choice, and a damned smart one at that.

After recounting my tale of self-publishing to Gillian, it was plain to see that she realised that too. With a slow and deliberate motion, she reached into her bag and withdrew a little notebook and a chewed-up pen. That moment was a special one, I'll tell you that. It confirmed to me what I had been striving for all along – that I was as valid as any of the authors surrounding me, stacked on the tall shelves.

Let's just say that I stayed in that chair for at least another hour and that Gillian left tightly clutching her notebook and my business card, her perceptions changed, full of new ideas, and already itching to know more…

…And I would wager that's why you picked up this Complete Guide.

You've made a good choice.

You may be here because you have just put the final bit of punctuation on the final page of your debut and now you're keen to show it off to the world.

Or, you might have just leapt into your first chapter and are full to bursting with ideas and dreams of how far you can take it. (The sky's the limit, I'll tell you that.)

Or, you may be an established traditional author, looking for more control over your books, and better royalties while you're at it.

Whatever sort of author you are, you've come to the right place.

If you delve into the history of self-publishing, you'll soon find that the concept isn't an entirely new one. Mark Twain self-published his works. As did Virginia Woolf. And let's not forget good old Benjamin Franklin. What is new, however, is the age that we now live in. A downright brilliant age if you ask me.

We live in the glorious age of digital publishing, a time where technology and market forces have come together, and gifted us authors with the chance to succeed without the help of a traditional publishing house. Self-publishing has now moved on from tiresome 'vanity publishing' – a phrase which evokes visions of authors standing at the doors of their garages, glaring at piles of unsold books. No longer do we have to traipse from one bookshop to the next, selling a copy here, a copy there. For the first time in history, and thanks to our good friend, the internet, we can sell and deliver content in multiple formats all over the world and without even having to get off our couches. We can chat to our fans *en masse* or one-on-one without putting on our shoes. Technology has built a new breed of author. The self-publisher. The indie. The "author-preneur".

So what does this all mean, my fellow pen-jockey? It means you've entered the market at a great time, possibly the best time. This new market is a voracious one and now we have the tools to feed it. With hard work, passion, and a good dollop of know-how, you've got a shot at achieving that dream of being a successful professional author. So if you've got the passion and are ready for some hard work, then I've got the know-how. I approach self-publishing from a DIY perspective, which means taking the reins with your own hands. I call it the Shelf Help method, and this guide will tell you all about it. But firstly, here's a little introduction to who I am, and why I've written this guide.

A little introduction

I spent most of my young life with my nose buried in a book and, as all authors know, reading and writing are very much intertwined. By the time I turned twelve I had just finished my very first book and was already moving on to my second. Thankfully, they never saw, and never will see, the light of day, but unbeknownst to me, these books formed the foundation of the author I am today.

At that time, in the late 1990s, there was very little self-publishing information available and very few self-publishing tools existed. The only real path to major success that existed for budding authors at that time was traditional publishing – polishing your manuscript, finding an agent, submitting your baby to a publishing house, and crossing your fingers very tightly. There was of course vanity publishing, but since I clueless about either option, and distracted by school and the trappings of teen-hood, my dream of becoming an author remained exactly that: a dream. I kept on scribbling, but my stories never left the screen, or escaped the notepad.

Then, in 2009, it all changed. I'd spent the last two years studying bass guitar at a music academy whilst working an endless succession of dead-end jobs in pubs, bars and hot pasty kiosks. As I hopped from job to job, the hours seemed to get longer and the tasks more tedious. Every new job seemed the same. A year on from the academy, I was fed up with serving drinks and felt that my music career was never going to get off the ground. I realised it was time for a change. I wanted out – and badly. That old dream of mine had been reignited.

So I wrote a book.

That book was called *The Written* and it is the reason I'm here today, writing this very paragraph. The idea for *The Written* materialised, as all good ideas do, completely out of thin air, and practically grabbed me by the throat. It was to be an epic fantasy, perhaps the start of a series, full of action and magic and myth. Brutal. Dark. Emotional. All wrapped up in one.

And so it was. I wrote it in the evenings, in the mornings, on weekends, between shifts, and even during shifts, writing on my mobile phone whenever I got a moment between customers. Words came and went and eighteen months later, in early 2010, I had what resembled a finished book, almost ready to be unleashed on the world. Boy, was I proud! There was only one question: how the hell would I publish the thing?

My route to market was one paved with a lot of research and much trial and error. My original plan was to publish in the traditional way, but while I was combing through Google for agents, I spotted a banner describing something called 'self-publishing'. The concept seemed too good to be true. Over the next few months, as I put the finishing touches to *The Written*, I read everything on self-publishing I could get my hands on. It was a steep learning curve, but I dug up everything I had learnt at the music academy – marketing skills, professionalism and a handful of technical know-how – and turned it around so I could apply it to my book. Fortunately for me, the publishing and music industries are very similar indeed, and a lot of the knowledge transferred quite nicely. If I had missed the boat with music, I was on the cusp of the wave with books. So after a lot of work, in early 2011, not only was a book published, but the Shelf Help method was born too.

The Written quickly led to book number two, *Pale Kings*, secretly my favourite out of all 'The Emaneska Series'. I wrote that book in a hundred days, and published it in early 2012. In turn the Shelf Help method was refined again, this time to be slicker and simpler. After *Pale Kings* flew off the drawing board in record time, I recognised that I had a method that worked, and that it was time to share it with the world. I knew for a fact that there were other budding writers out there who, like me, were eager to escape the banality of a job that wasn't writing. When I first published, information and good advice were scarce, so I wanted to change that and to show others the way. By that time, I was already beginning to speak about self-publishing at universities and conferences, but I knew I needed to go bigger and wider, so I could reach more authors. I needed another website. And so, sitting on the dusty steps of the London Book Fair in 2012, I found myself excitedly typing two words into my laptop: *Shelf Help*. My advice website was born.

Thanks to Shelf Help and my experiences as an indie author, I now work as a self-publishing consultant, helping all sorts of authors and companies understand self-publishing. Shelf Help has aided a great many authors since its launch in August 2012, and every little bit of feedback has spurred me on to provide more, to do more. This is why I wrote this guide, and why I hope it helps you. It's certainly a method that works! 'The Emaneska Series', now four books strong, is finished and a graphic novel version of *The Written* is due for launch in early 2014. I've also taken another step in supporting authors by co-founding the indie-only eBook store Libiro, which flies the flag of self-publishing 24/7. The reason I'm able to do all this? Self-publishing. How can I not help but shout about it?

Now that you know my self-publishing tale, I hope it has been interesting to see what has led me here, what has inspired me. I humbly hope it inspires you. Anyway, that's enough about me. Let's learn more about how this guide can help you.

The purpose of this handy guide

Let's be frank. This is not a guide to making millions. Nor is it a guide to getting rich quick. Nor is it intended to be an easy fix or a short cut. Speaking honestly, self-publishing is hard work. Being an author is a job. A dream job, of course, but a job nonetheless!

By 2008, sales of the Harry Potter books had reached the 400 million mark. Was JK Rowling an overnight success? No. She started writing *Harry Potter and the Philosopher's Stone* in 1990, and it took her 5 years to write it, battling against unemployment and family crises. When she was finally picked up by the thirteenth publisher that she and her agent approached, she wasn't offered seven figures, nor six, nor even five. **Instead, JK was paid a modest £1500 for her troubles.** It took another two books and another four years to truly hit the big time, in 2000, when *Goblet of Fire* broke sales records in both the US and the UK. What does this mean? It means that JK Rowling worked and worked hard for her success. It means that she had two things working in her favour – a damned good story to tell and a solid work ethic. Like JK, these are two elements that you, the author, need to bring to the table.

But what about the know-how? That's where Shelf Help comes in. This guide won't show you how to make a fortune overnight (indeed, I don't believe any guide on this earth can), but what it will aim to do is give you the knowledge and skills needed to get your book published and to become a sustainable business – to become a professional indie author.

This guide will show you **how to publish the Shelf Help way**, and how to stay true to the method's three pillars, which we'll discuss in a moment. As I've mentioned, mine is a DIY approach. By taking the reins yourself, you retain your rights, your royalties and your creative control, and that's the beauty of DIY self-publishing.

A quick note on: *Self-Publishing _ a misnomer*

Now it's wise to mention here that the term 'self-publishing' is actually a little bit of a misnomer. As we'll see in the following pages, the DIY approach involves hiring and outsourcing professionals, so in essence, we indies hardly ever publish by ourselves. But we do keep control. As such, self-publishing, although it has become the most popular term, isn't actually the most accurate term. Many authors and organisations, such as the Alliance of Independent Authors, call it "author-publishing" or "indie publishing" instead. These terms may be more accurate, but for the purposes of simplicity and comfort, we'll be referring to the indie process as "self-publishing" throughout this guide. I hope that helps!

Shelf Help will **demystify this DIY approach** and show you in a methodical, step-by-step way how to go from an unedited manuscript to that very first royalty cheque. I'll give you the knowledge necessary to create a product that you will be proud to publish, then I'll show you how to publish and sell this product correctly, affordably and with maximum effect. In doing so, using my tips and tricks, I will get you on that inside track and help you stay ahead of the competition. Although it does depend on the quality of the book you've written, Shelf Help will give you the professional edge that is vital to give yourself a chance at success.

This guide will also **let you shake hands with the industry** and introduce you to the field upon which the self-publishing game is played. You will meet the players who play it – something that is essential if you're going to be joining in.

This guide will show you how to navigate the twisting and ever-changing landscape of publishing and, hopefully, stay future-safe.

So that's what this book can do for you. Excited? I am. Let's move on and look at the three pillars that govern the Shelf Help method.

The Three Pillars of Shelf Help self-publishing

There are three pillars of the Shelf Help method – three over-arching concepts that define how we should approach self-publishing today, tomorrow and in the future. Here they are:

Affordability

Affordability is important to new authors, just like it is to today's digital start-up companies. By keeping initial and ongoing costs low, authors can maximise return – breaking even earlier and therefore having a better chance to make a living. Some of us may publish just for the love and passion of writing, but most publish seeking a viable career and that means being aware of costs and thinking like a business!

Professionalism

Professionalism is paramount to shaking off the unfortunate self-publishing stigma that is now attributed to indie authors. Although the stigma is slowly waning, many readers see self-published books as low-quality and not worth the time of day. This is primarily due to the huge amount of eager authors who rushed into the industry at the dawn of the self-publishing revolution when technology first changed the whole publishing game. A large number of these authors spent neither time nor money striving for a professional standard and so unfortunately we authors of today must work a little harder to stand apart. I'll be showing you how to attain these high standards later.

Technology

Lastly, a technology-driven approach. Technology started this revolution and it hasn't let up since. We authors now have access to all sorts of different tools that can help us reach readers and make a viable living. Thanks to eBooks and eReaders, indie authors can now publish to a global audience at the click of a button. Thanks to print-on-demand publishing technology, we can now sell print books at affordable prices. Thanks to social media, we can now talk to our readers in real-time, from all over the world. It's important we learn how to use these twenty-first-century platforms, to give ourselves the best chance of success in the future.

How this guide is structured

First, we'll look at the industry as a whole – its history, its current landscape and where self-publishing fits in.

After this, we'll break the self-publishing journey into three simple steps. Like the three pillars of the Shelf Help method, the DIY process is divided into the three parts. The three P's:

Polish it.
Publish it.
Promote it.

Think of these steps as a **before** (getting your book ready for publishing), a **during** (the upload and pressing of the 'publish' button) and an **after** (the promotion and marketing of your book). We'll examine each in turn.

We'll then close with three Q&A sessions with fellow self-publishing experts and professional authors: Hugh Howey, Polly Courtney and Joanna Penn.

Now that you know where we're headed, it's time to get going! First stop: **the industry**.

The
Industry

A History of Publishing

Once upon a time, there was a publishing industry. It was very different to the one we know today, but it's the reason we're here. That's why I believe it's very important to learn about it. As a wise man once said:

'How can you know where you're going if you don't know where you've come from?'

We humans have always been obsessed with scribbling things. Written language was born over 3000 years ago when Mesopotamians carved characters into tablets of moist clay and Egyptians from the First Dynasty dribbled ink across papyrus. These first languages were devoted to chronicling man's achievements, another one of our natural obsessions. Soon enough, usage of these tablets and papyrus sheets began to increase rapidly. The written word began to spread and soon, scholars and scribes began to get ambitious. It wasn't long before codices and scrolls were born – huge collections of individual notes and passages. They were deemed so important that they were buried with kings, or kept in temples and great libraries. This was the genesis of what we know today as the humble book. The very beginning.

Parchment – invented by the Greeks – soon followed in the wake of clay and papyrus. Paper came too, invented in China around the second century BC. Around that time, methods of printing slowly crept into existence. Early books began to circulate and a brand new culture bubbled up around them. This was publishing in an embryonic state.

If our ancestors in the second century BC paved the way, those of the Renaissance would inject it with life.

In the twelfth century AD, the shadow of the dark ages had been thrown aside, and a new age had begun. Art, music, learning, literature – they were all experiencing a rebirth. The human race had developed a voracious hunger for learning, one that hadn't been felt since the Roman Empire had fallen. Books began to escape from the monasteries and made their way into the city streets, into the hands of the common man and woman. Universities across Europe began to produce their own manuscripts for their students and teachers. Private libraries began to abound. The price of paper, imported from China and the Arab world, decreased. As the world moved on from innovation to innovation, so did the book.

Where there's innovation, there's industry. The greatest leap forward for the book was the invention of the printing press in 1440, by Mr Johannes Gutenberg. It applied what would become an industrial process to the humble, treasured book.

Thanks to the printing press, printed literature soon began to spread through Europe and beyond like wild fire. Books quickly became a commodity to be sold and bought. Publishing began to establish itself as a business. In the mid-fifteenth century, the first ever book trade fair took place very near to where Mr Gutenberg printed his very first Bible – Frankfurt, in Germany. There's even an account of King Henry VIII sending an emissary to the fair to buy books for the new Oxford Library. To this day The Frankfurt Book Fair is still one of the biggest events on the publishing calendar.

When William Caxton produced the first book ever printed in English, in 1474-1475, it marked yet another momentous moment for the publishing industry. The first-ever English retailer of books, Caxton spent his time carefully selecting titles and used his own press to publish them to small but well-defined markets. Sound familiar? I bet it does. It was a notion that soon spread overseas. In 1638, when a printing press was imported to Cambridge, Massachusetts, America entered the book publishing arena with vigour. Printing pioneer Benjamin Franklin opened his own print shop in 1728, publishing the famous Pennsylvania Gazette as well as several books.

Slowly but surely, the publishing industry took the form we are so familiar with today.

In the nineteenth and twentieth centuries, early self-publishers emerged, paying the costs of their own printing and selling books by hand to readers and bookshops. Writers such as Mark Twain (whose publishing business actually bankrupted him), Lewis Carroll, Edgar Allen Poe, Rudyard Kipling, Walt Whitman, and Virginia Woolf all published their own books. The royalty system came into being, followed by international copyright protection, which made sure that authors got paid. And in 1817, a familiar name emerged in the publishing world: Harper. Major publishing houses were born, and over the next century and a half, the publishing industry grew to utterly staggering proportions. So successful was it that in the year 2000, publishing houses in the United States generated nearly $25bn (£15bn) in revenue. Together, they and others around the world held sway over what was published and what wasn't. What was popular and what had had its day. They were the guardians and the gatekeepers, and it was a very exclusive club indeed.

But it was then that this industry began to transform. Something called the internet had arrived and it looked set to stay. As technology went from strength to strength, advances in digital printing, digital reading and e-commerce led to a revolution in publishing. The power moved quickly from the conglomerate to the individual. This industry of closed doors and gatekeepers was thrown wide open, and an age of author-entrepreneurs was born. Self-publishing had arrived.

The Digital Revolution and the rise of self-publishing

When speaking about the digital revolution, a great parallel can be drawn between the music industry and the book industry. The music industry saw its own digital revolution when the MP3 waded into consumers' lives. By the late 1990s, the MP3's convenient file size and the ease of sharing it over the good old internet meant that independent artists and bands could reach their fans directly. More importantly, they could actually make a living out of it. The effect of this? A decreased dependence on the all-powerful major record labels and therefore a rise in successful independent media. That's exactly what's happened for us authors in our own industry.

Fast-forward a few years and the eBook (accompanied of course by its vital partner, the eReader) had begun to make waves in the book industry. The internet swooped in to save the day again. As it became easier and more commonplace to transmit and sell files over the internet, consumers' tastes shifted. The age of the eBook had arrived.

What did this mean? Hopeful authors, who may have been heading down the traditional path of finding an agent and submitting manuscripts to publishers, suddenly found a gap in the fence – a way to bypass the big houses and reach readers directly. In other words, the gatekeepers no longer guarded all the gates.

Authors could now use the internet to sell eBooks directly to readers, anywhere around the connected globe. All those well-established and traditional distribution channels were suddenly side-lined. Via email, websites, online marketing and an increasingly popular thing called social media, authors found they could take control of their own success. We could publish with no agents, no publishers, and without most of the drawbacks of earlier self-publishing models. Hooray for the internet!

But there were a few things missing from the twenty-first-century author's toolkit. Access, for one – direct access to the big online stores and major bookshops. But the rise of independent authors had been noticed. In 2007, the Kindle was launched, and with it came Kindle Direct Publishing. KDP was ground-breaking – a direct link straight into what could be described as the biggest online store in history. Every self-publishing author could now take a shot at the big time, competing side-by-side with the traditional crowd.

Other stores soon opened their doors, notably Barnes & Noble, when they launched their own self-publishing platform PubIt! in 2010. (Yes, that exclamation mark is compulsory, though it's now been renamed 'Nook Press'.) The self-publishing landscape quickly became a busy place, packed full of eager indie authors and providers that had popped up to satisfy the demand for writing, publishing, and marketing services. Self-publishing had made its entrance – and in style. Author after author leapt into the fray. So much so in fact, that in 2009, 76% of all books published in that year were self-published. That, in my opinion, is incredible. A historical moment for publishing and for authors.

But I should warn you: it hasn't been the easiest road and there are cons to the self-publishing process. Primarily, we miss out on that all-important advance. In bypassing a publisher, we must rely on building up the income ourselves. It also means that funding the publishing becomes our responsibility (however, as I'm about to show you, it can be deceptively affordable if done right!). There are also another two problems that have plagued self-publishing from the beginning:

Stigma

The first problem is the self-publishing stigma, as it's come to be called. Simply put, some readers believe that because a book hasn't been published by a traditional house, it must, therefore, be talentless tripe. Of course, we all know this isn't true. Or is it? Well sadly, it's partially true. There is a double-edge to self-publishing and it is this: when you can publish anything, people will publish *anything*. I'll be frank with you, there is a lot of rubbish out there. A lot of tripe. Whether it's authors simply not knowing any better, or authors being lazy, it's given the whole lot of us a bad reputation. This is why we now must work a little harder to shrug off that misconception. But don't worry, we'll be discussing how it's done very shortly.

The other problem is this:

Every ecosystem has its predators

The self-publishing industry is no exception. Our predators are the companies that brand themselves as one-stop self-publishing shops, sometimes known as 'package providers'. You can normally spot them quite easily. They're the ones with cleverly named packages like 'The Sovereign Package' or the 'Platinum Package', which incidentally carry price tags of anywhere up to $16,000.

To perch on the soapbox for a spell (and fear not, I'll get off it soon), these companies treat authors like items on a conveyor belt, putting the authors on the financial back foot with their high prices. If we are to be businesses, then we need low start-up costs. A huge $16,000 investment before you've even had a single sale is not a wise business decision. Remember the first Shelf Help pillar? ***Affordability!***

The true shame of it is that these providers behave as if they were the only publishing solutions available to authors. It would be great if they were all author-centric and top-notch, but they're not. Instead they offer what I consider to be average or downright dire services, making it even harder than normal to recoup that large initial investment. Profit abruptly becomes a distant object.

I've had run-ins with many of these companies in the past and can only say it's like dealing with car salesmen. The authors that unfortunately get sucked into their system often pay a high price, such as in the case of Vantage Press.

When Vantage Press collapsed in 2012, a lot of authors were left reeling in its rubble. Vantage Press was one of these package providers. You see, these companies take a lot of the DIY out of DIY publishing. They handle the editing, the cover design, the publishing, but most importantly, they manage the distribution, stock and your royalties. When a company handles that much of your book empire, you're only as strong as the company. When the company breaks, as Vantage Press did under the strain of a poor financial climate, you break too. Vantage authors suddenly found themselves without stock, royalty cheques, distribution channels, or any information whatsoever. In the end authors had to release Vantage of all debts and unpaid royalties. Stock that wasn't claimed by the authors (who actually had to pay to have it shipped to them) was sold off by Vantage to cover their losses. Not a penny or a cent was seen by many authors. Most of them were back to square one, and I've helped many of them back onto their feet since Vantage dissolved. This is why I believe that DIY is always the best step forward.

I don't mean to wax cautionary on this subject, but it wouldn't be right to guide you along a road without pointing out the potholes. In my time helping others publish, I've heard dozens of stories about authors falling foul of these companies. I simply won't allow you to do the same!

So what companies can you trust? I'll be introducing some of them to you as we move forward. For the rest, once you see how professional and affordable the Shelf Help method can be, and get deep into the mind-set of a business, you'll automatically be wary and wise of any giant price tag.

Stats

I think it's high time we put these incredible advances in technology and sweeping market change into numbers, don't you? That way we can really appreciate the publishing headlines of the last few years.

Fact No. 1: eBooks are here to stay, thanks to a rise in available content and advances in eReading technology.

Between January and June 2011, eBook sales rose 623%.
The world had adopted eBooks with open arms.

Fact No. 2: The industry is now focusing on digital sales and their e-catalogues, as well as new forms of content – just like us self-publishers!

£50m

£1m

2011   2012

Publishing house Hachette reported digital sales of £50m in 2012. This is compared to £1m, in 2011.

Fact No. 3: It isn't just a reading and writing revolution in the US and the UK – it's gone global now.

In 2012, the Japanese eBook market was reported to be worth **$741m** *(USD)*

Authors using the eBook publishing platform Kobo Writing Life have published works in over 138 countries and in 50 languages

Fact No. 4: We self-publishers are here to stay. There are now more of us publishing books than ever before.

Between 2011 and 2012, there was a 59% increase in self-published titles in the US – this equates to a massive 391,000 titles. (And it doesn't even take into account books published without an ISBN, such as on Amazon!)

Fact No. 5: We're not just for show, we're selling books too, and in large amounts!

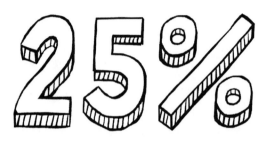

In December 2013, Amazon revealed that 25% of the Kindle books sold in 2012 were self-published via Kindle Direct Publishing.

Fact No. 6: The market is voracious – and digital too.

Of Americans now own an eReading device such as a Nook, a Kindle or a tablet.

in

Britons now own
an eReader

So in summary...

Altogether, looking at the history of the digital revolution and those statistics, it's easy to see that it's an exciting time for us authors. Opportunity abounds. The consumer is voracious. It's a perfect storm of technology and market forces. Yes, the industry has been turned on its head and the landscape changes weekly, but whether this is a good or a bad thing depends on who and what you are. We're authors, and I look at those statistics and say there's never been a better time to publish. That excites me and I'm sure it excites you too. So now that you know the field and its players, it's time to play the game itself.

Part 1 | *Polish It*

Why your manuscript simply won't do

Once you put the final punctuation on that final page, congratulations are in order. You've done something great. Some of you may have written this book for yourself, simply for the challenge, but the rest of you will be keen to publish your masterpiece. Unfortunately, you can't just click publish once you've finished your book – there's a little more work to be done yet! Why? Because your book isn't in a format you can sell. It may contain mistakes. It doesn't have a cover. It is most likely in a Word or Pages format. We need to do a little more work before you hit the stores.

In this section we'll be looking at the first P in the Shelf Help process: **Polishing**. This is the process of transforming your manuscript into a professional, sellable product, one that can help you compete with the rest of the market, and one that will help you make a living.

We'll be looking at three key tasks here: the **editing** of your words and your story, the creation of a **cover** for your book, and the **formatting** of your manuscript, so it can be printed and/or sold as an eBook.

Let's look at Editing first.

Editing

Editing. That word may send shivers through many of you. This is usually for two reasons: perhaps it has a reputation for being a difficult task, or perhaps you've heard horror stories of how much it can cost. But fear not! In this first section, I will be breaking editing down into easy chunks and showing you two affordable ways of polishing up that book of yours.

But first, let's discuss *why* you need to edit your book.

Why you need to edit your book

Almost every single book in history has experienced a reshuffle, or a little re-write here and there. This is because things are rarely perfect on the first go, or the second, or even the third. Think of it like this – why polish a table? Why season a soup? Why carve a diamond? Because as impressive as they might already be, there is a possibility they can be made better. Our books are no exception. As authors, we owe it to ourselves and to our prospective fans to make sure our books are as perfect as they can possibly be. If we are going to be professional authors then we really need to be turning out professional products.

So what exactly is editing? Well, as our good ol' friend Wikipedia puts it:

'Editing is the process of selecting and preparing written, visual, audible and film media used to convey information through the processes of correction, condensation, organisation and other modifications performed with an intention of producing a correct, consistent, accurate and complete work.'

The key words in that sentence are '**consistent**, **accurate** and **complete**'. All of these are elements of professionalism and perfection, and all of these can help you sell books. That's why they are important!

Some of you may believe that editing simply applies to spotting typos and fixing grammatical mistakes. Editing is more than that. It actually applies to every single ingredient in your book: its flow, characters, plot, execution, continuity, grammar, spelling and even the structure as a whole. This means that there is also more than one type of editor. Some editors you come across will be all-rounders, but others will specialise in specific types of editing – copy editors, line editors, and developmental editors, for example.

Editing, therefore, is a major step in the book publishing process. Without editing your book you run the risk of plot-holes, embarrassing typos, and even worse, poor reviews and bad sales, all of which punch very large and jagged holes in your chances of success.

This is the crux of editing. Your readers will expect your book to be error-free and well-written. They will expect this for two reasons: one, because they have parted with money for it; and two, because traditional publishing houses have spent the last dozen decades working to put professionally edited books on the world's shelves. Of course, traditional books aren't always 100% perfect, but hey, traditional publishers are human too.

So when your debut book hits Amazon – un-edited, un-polished and raw – your first few paying customers might not be too happy when the typos start interrupting their reading and souring their enjoyment of your story. The result? Poor reviews, subsequently poor sales and perhaps even a confirmation for readers that self-published books aren't worth the money and the time after all. Remember – first impressions are important for your business as well as your reputation as an author. That's why you want to make sure you get it right the first time.

Lastly, don't forget that if errors do slip through the net and you discover them after you've published, making changes can cost money, especially with print publishing. Catching them now can save you money in the future!

Let's move on from the why to the how.

Ways of editing your book

Editing your book can be achieved via two methods:

- Using a professional editor,
- Or using beta-readers.

Wait just one moment: surely there's a third method, **editing it yourself**? Yes, that is an option, but it's one that comes with a warning:

True editing is a skill and a profession. The question I pose to you is: Is this you? Are you a professional editor? Are you able to stand back and see the bigger picture, to be objective and impartial, to be tough and critical, shrewd and honest? I would say that only a fraction of you truly is. Everybody can edit, in the sense of spotting errors, or re-writing the occasional paragraph, but I know I'm not an *editor*. I always say that I'm second-draft material – that's as far as my editing involvement goes! Now while it isn't uncommon for editors to write, or for writers to pick up editing skills along the way – to sharpen their eyes, so to speak – we're still too close to the book. That's why DIY editing can be dangerous.

The truth is that editing must be done without bias, and sadly very, very few authors can view their own book without bias. We are connected on an emotional level. It is why none of us like a bad review – we are invested in our own creations. It is human nature to be protective, to be fondly prejudiced. This might mean you can't bring yourself to trim the fat off that last chapter, or that you can't spot a weak section, or that your eyes, being attached to the brain that wrote the words, simply glide straight past mistakes without a second thought.

This is why it's wise to get a second pair of eyes involved.

Before any editing takes place...
...make sure you do a second draft of your book.

This is important for two reasons. The first is time. This is connected to the second: money. By producing a second draft, you complete a lot of the groundwork for your editor or beta readers. Therefore you're not wasting their time. And where a freelance editor is concerned, time means money.

Producing a second draft is an intrinsic part of the editing process, and helps you catch those silly little mistakes and typos that can easily be corrected without any help. It also helps you to get a better grasp of the structure and overall flow of your story, which means you can make any major changes before you start the external editing process. In other words, you'll be handing over a more complete and realised book to your editor or betas.

How you go about producing a second draft is completely up to you. Some of you may like to print it out and work through it with the good ol' red pen. Others may be happy trawling through text on-screen. Whatever is comfortable for you, being thorough is the key.

What I like to do is make several different types of notes when working on my second draft. Some are directly linked to the text (such as spelling errors or punctuation mistakes, others are concerning structure (whether a paragraph or chapter should by moved, reduced, or cut), and notes on general improvement. What also helps is reading each sentence slowly and out loud. This really helps you analyse the flow and pace of your prose.

Once you've got your second draft, make sure it's easy for your editor or betas to work with. Your second draft needn't look like the finished article. In fact, that can actually hamper the process. Instead, strip out all the formatting so that your editor/beta can get their teeth into the bare text. Sometimes, when using other word processors like Pages (as I do) formatting can be preserved and cause trouble. Make sure it's in a universal format, such as a Word file (.doc). Also make sure that the line spacing is wide and easy to read (for example, double-space), and that the fonts are large and simple enough. You can never go wrong with Times New Roman in eleven- or twelve-point font. It may make your book look a little stark, but you get to put all the formatting back in at the formatting and typesetting stages.

Now let's look at the two types of editing method available to us authors.

Freelance Editors

Although using a professional editor comes at a cost, I always say that it's a wise investment, and one of the few important first investments you should make as a self-publishing author. Good, professional editors will have spent years honing their skills and their objective eye, so their focused attention on your book can pay dividends when you come to publish.

What professional editors do is intensively close-read your book and highlight changes that they think need to be made. They don't normally make final changes to the text; that's your job. Pro editors work in tandem with the author, applying their skills as well as objectivity. It's for this reason that you'll see authors thanking their editor or editors in dedications, for all their help and good advice. Pro editors should have an advanced grasp of language and grammar, possibly creative writing skills of their own, an uncanny ability to see the bigger picture and understand your style, and a knowledge of trends and the market.

That may sound like a difficult person to find, but fear not. With the popularity of self-publishing still sky-rocketing and publishers down-sizing, the demand for and the supply of editors has naturally increased. This is great news, as it means it's now relatively easy to find a freelance editor (or editors) who can help you. Now, there are a few aspects to be aware of when setting out to find yourself an editor. These range from the types of editing available, how much it costs, how to approach an editor and also how to work with an editor. Let's discuss these.

The different types of editing

Editors aren't all the same, nor do they all do the exact same job. As we discussed earlier, there are different types of editing:

- Developmental editing relates to substantial structural changes to the story, its characters, or its setting. This might mean rewriting, adding or omitting whole chapters.
- Editing grammar, sentence structure, punctuation and layout is called copy-editing or line editing.
- Proofreading comes at the end of the process, and involves a final sweep to pick up any final remaining errors like typos or wandering punctuation.

This means it's important to know what you want before you go out and get it. What sort of editing do you need? Do you need help with the story development or structure, or rather somebody to clean up your manuscript? Note your requirements down and write yourself a little brief. Then, when you start searching, you'll have a list of tick-boxes that any prospective pros have to fulfil.

How to find the right editor

Google may be your obvious choice, but I warn against it. Googling 'freelance book editor', last time I checked returned 17,200,000 results, and those were muddied by paid ads from big and possibly untrustworthy companies. Unless you're using some very specific Google search terms, I would suggest going by word of mouth and recommendation.

If you're part of an author's community, such as the **Alliance of Independent Authors**, then ask your fellow members to recommend a good editor. It's very likely that you'll end up with a list of possible candidates.

Another way of finding a good pro editor is to use resources such as the **Editorial Freelancers Association** in the USA or the **Society for Editors and Proofreaders** in the UK. Both organisations have directories of professionals, as well as forums where you can post jobs and ask questions. There are also guidelines and further advice on offer too.

Once you think you've found your editor, it's time to do a little research. If you can, talk to a previous client to find out whether they were happy with the work done. Also, see if you can get a reference from the editor. Beware the editor who is reticent to provide one.

Approaching an editor

When approaching your chosen editor, bear in mind that each will have his or her own way of working. Some editors might want to edit your book on good old-fashioned paper, others might be happy making notes on a PDF or Word document. Some editors will accept any genre under the sun; others might only specialise in sci-fi zombie romance. As we said earlier: every editor is different!

The acceptance of your work will also depend on your timescales, the editor's cost, and the size of your project. Don't be offended if an editor says no – it's good that they are being honest and upfront. It's much better to have an editor that's passionate about your book than one who has reservations and doubts.

Don't forget that the acceptance of your work will also depend on your introduction. It's time to screw your business head on tight. Make sure your introductory email or call is polite, friendly, detailed yet succinct, and above all, professional. Deliver all the information that the editor will need in one fell swoop so that neither party's time is wasted.

What you want to see is a spark between you. I'm not talking about a romantic spark here, not at all! I'm talking about a spark of like-mindedness. You're looking for enthusiasm and an instant understanding of where you're coming from. If you don't find it, be mindful of the fact that you could be working very closely with each other and baring the innards of your manuscript. If you don't feel 100% comfortable at the beginning, it may be detrimental to the process.

The cost of a pro

Cost can be a difficult thing to pin down when it comes to editing. Just as every author and book is different, so is every independent professional editor! More than likely, you will receive a quote in one of two forms: an hourly rate, or a quote based on word-count.

Quoting by word count can sometimes be a little unreliable, especially for the editor. If you've rushed your second draft, you might have worked harder on the first parts of your book, so the quality might drop as the pages progress. Therefore, the pace at which your editor can work may slow as he or she progresses. On the other hand, being tied into a fixed figure might occasionally create a temptation to rush the final chapters, and so you might not get exactly what you paid for.

From an author's perspective, if you've spent a lot of time polishing your book as much as possible before it goes to an editor, a word count quote might negate this effort – your book might not need a large amount of input from an editor, but word count quotes disregard this. Quoting by the hour is therefore a more balanced way of paying for editing, for both you and the editor. It will ensure that you, the author, gets the editor's undivided attention throughout the edit.

Now, let's expand on the concept of polishing up your manuscript *before* you send it to an editor. As we discussed earlier, doing a second and even third draft before handing your book over to an editor can reduce both the cost and time spent. One determining factor behind an editor's cost is what is being demanded of them. If the manuscript is 'clean', then it will need less work. So, before popping your book over to your chosen pro editor, pass it through the spell-checker, print it out and read then re-read it to check it is free of spelling and grammar mistakes. This means that your editor can work more quickly and focus on issues of style and reviewing the novel as a whole.

Another determining factor of cost is the editor's prior experience. If they're particularly brilliant, then they may just charge a bit extra for their time. It's the good old adage of:

'You get what you pay for!'

The Society for Editors and Proofreaders provide a few guidelines that are really helpful when gauging how much of your budget to use up. The SfEP's suggested minimum rates, revised every year, currently start at £21.40 ($35) per hour for proofreading and up to £28.80 ($48) per hour for developmental editing. This is only a guideline of course, and please do bear in mind that if you go after the industry's top editors, you'll likely pay a lot more!

How to work with your editor

The best advice here is to attempt to establish a good and frank relationship with your editor, but consciously keep a certain distance during the process. In other words, an open and honest professional relationship. You don't want to distract your busy editor with personal concerns, or nerves, or idle conversation. Instead, just let them focus and remain objective. Keep it succinct and businesslike. This is why conversing with your editor is usually best done via email, perhaps with the occasional feedback session over Skype. Just remember, with email you also have a record of your conversations, so you can refer back if needed.

Also bear in mind that this will be a commercial relationship. You're the buyer, the editor is the seller. You've swapped cash for services, so you need to make sure you're getting what you're paying for. Just be careful not to be too overly demanding, and keep any expectations realistic.

It's also important to be prepared. The editor will be critiquing your book. Trust me, I know that when you've spent the last few months or years working on a book, pouring your mind and emotion into it, you may find it difficult to hand it over to a stranger and watch them pick it apart. Here's the golden rule:

OPEN UP.

You might rankle at a few suggestions here and there, but it's very, very important to stay open to your editor's recommendations. It is his or her job, after all. It's what you're paying for. You have the right to disagree, but before you do, make sure you understand the reasons behind your editor's suggestion, so that you can make an informed decision. Have a little discussion to really analyse the whys and wherefores. It's also good practice for the future too, just in case you should get a bad review!

And that's my guide to freelance editing. Now, if you want to try an alternate approach, one with a different cost model altogether, then you may be interested in getting some:

Beta Readers

Beta reading is a unique way of getting your book edited – a technique we indie authors borrowed from the video game and software industries.

Before a developer can release a new game or app, they test it to make sure it runs correctly and that it will have every chance of being well-received by its audience. (Already sounds a little familiar, doesn't it?) One stage of this testing is called 'beta testing', a process where test versions of the software are released to a limited audience outside of the development team. This audience, normally composed of small and experienced groups, tests the software and offers feedback in an effort to work out all the bugs and faults. It's like they say:

'Many hands make light work.'

And we can do the same with our manuscripts.

Beta reading is done by asking a small yet concentrated community of readers to edit and proofread your book. Like editors, they won't make corrections, but instead suggest them as well as give overall feedback about the story and its flow.

The most important thing about beta reading is that it's voluntary and therefore largely free. Now there's a great word, especially to a first-time author. I've used beta readers for all four of my books and all my betas have ever asked for in return is a few signed copies and a mention in the books, both of which I'm more than happy to give. But is beta reading as good as freelance editing? I believe it can be – you just have to find the right betas. More on this in a moment.

This is the beauty of beta reading. It's perfectly symbiotic. Like crowd-sourcing, or crowd-funding, betas get front-row seats – they get to be part of the project and the process. They get the chance to work with an author directly and they get to read your latest book without paying a penny – usually months before anybody else. It's that novelty that you, the author, bring to the table. In return, and if you go about it the right way, you get an edited, polished product in return, at a fraction of the cost of a freelance editor.

But how exactly do we go about recruiting beta readers? Luckily, the practice is becoming quite a common one. Many readers are now aware of the opportunity to beta-read, and many actually approach authors directly if they catch the scent of a new book in the works. That's how I found most of my current betas.

However, for a debut author, you may not yet have the following or presence, so the task of searching falls to you. Now, there are a few things to bear in mind when recruiting betas. Like finding the right editor, you need to find the right sort of beta. Contrary to popular belief, not just anyone can be a beta reader. More specifically, not just anyone can be your beta reader. It's not quite as simple as finding twenty of your friends on Facebook and sending them your book. Nor is it a simple matter of sending a crowd of people your book and waiting for the edits to roll in. You need to go about this carefully, patiently, and professionally.

The first step is finding your betas.

How to find your beta readers

What sort of people should you be looking for? Here's a list of traits I believe are essential for betas.

1. **Honesty.** Editing is not a time for yes-men and biased feedback. You're looking for accurate and impartial suggestions. In other words, you're looking for people who are not afraid to speak their mind. Honesty also means being trustworthy. You should be able to trust your betas with an unfinished, and therefore private, piece of work.

2. **Great grammar and spelling.** It's no good having betas who can't spell, nor those who don't know their 'there' from their 'their'. Your betas need to be red-hot where language and prose are concerned. Otherwise those errors will pass by unnoticed.

3. **A pinch of creative talent.** Like a professional editor, your beta readers should have some creative bones in their bodies, preferably creative writing bones. This way, they won't just point out the mistakes; they'll be able to offer good suggestions too.

4. **Experience of your genre.** Make sure your betas are comfortable and familiar with your chosen genre. Otherwise, it may cause confusion, and simply make your betas' jobs harder. Bear in mind: betas are volunteers. You want to keep the process as easy and as enjoyable as possible, so if they're romance

fans, they probably won't want to trawl through half a chapter of Elvish poetry.

5. **Easy to work with.** Lastly, it's important to find betas who are easy to work with, people who won't be put out when you decide not to take their suggestions on board. If you think back to the recent discussion on how to work with a freelance editor, you can use the same guidelines.

So there's your mould. Now we just need to find some people to fill it! Don't worry – I've put together a few tips on how to find yourself the right type of person.

Amazon and Goodreads

Trawl both these websites. They are great places to find prospective betas, and the reason for this is that these two sites are hotbeds of reviewing action. Amazon, the largest online store in the world, thrives on user reviews. By actively facilitating and encouraging reviews, they've created a culture unto itself – a culture of seasoned readers, well-versed in speaking their mind on aspects such as genre and prose. These are the sorts of people you want to talk to: those who a) frequently leave reviews for books similar to yours in both style and genre; and b) leave honest constructive and detailed feedback – not overly critical or abusive.

Professionals

Teachers, professors, copywriters, journalists and other authors – there's a good chance you know at least one out of that list. And even if you don't, you'll probably know somebody who does, or be able to unearth a few of these betas on Facebook. These sorts of professionals will have a good knowledge of grammar, spelling and hopefully a creative streak in them too. If they're willing, they can make great betas.

Fans

You might already have published a few books in your time, or maybe a short story or two. If this is you, then you may already have a fan base of your own. Whether you've got a veritable army of fans, or just a scattering of followers, there's a good chance you'll be able to find a few betas in their midst. Look out for the people who are eager to get in touch with you and tell you what they think of your work, and keep a special eye out for the fans who make a few suggestions as to what you might be able to improve. They're the ones to reach out to!

A quick note on: *friends and family*

Friends and family might be the obvious choice when trying to find betas, but be cautious. You're looking for honest and unbiased feedback, and therefore betas you know very well might not be most impartial betas on offer. This isn't to say that all your friends and family are liars! Not at all. Rather that they might be reticent to hurt your feelings. These people have watched you slave away over a hot laptop or notepad for months on end. They know what this book means to you and therefore may not jump at the chance to poke holes in it. Of course, you know your friends and family better than anybody. Only you will be able to decide if they make great betas or not. I'll leave that to you! Just bear in mind the necessary traits we discussed earlier.

But how many beta readers will I need?

That's a very good question! I always suggest a minimum of six. This will ensure that you get a wide enough spectrum of feedback and it also covers your back should anybody unfortunately back out. It does happen!

I would also suggest a maximum of twelve to fifteen betas. With these numbers, it can be hard to keep track of who's handed in their notes and who hasn't, and you might end up giving yourself more work than you'd bargained for.

Rounding up your betas

When the good old to-do list gets a bit too big for its boots, or when I'm trying to do half a dozen things at once, you might have seen me tweeting something along the lines of:

'It's as easy as herding cats.'

It's one of my favourite sayings, but it should never describe your beta reading experience. Here are a few tricks for making sure your betas are briefed and organised, and ensuring that the whole process is as smooth as an infant's posterior.

1. **Second draft.** As with freelance editing, before you do anything at all, make sure you go back through your book and refine it into a second draft. Once again, this an important stage that helps you weed out all those easy-to-spot errors and stops you from wasting your beta readers' valued time. It also helps you firm up your overall plot and the structure of the book. It's vital to do this before handing over to a beta. Otherwise you might change your mind halfway through the beta-reading process and you definitely don't want to make your betas start all over again. Don't forget to make it easy to read as well – stripping out formatting, increasing the line spacing

and exporting it in a universal format like Word (.Doc).

2. **Make a list and check it twice.** Make a master list of all your prospective betas, so you can take notes on who's on board, and who's not, and also keep track of their progress during the process.

3. **Get in touch.** When you first reach out to your betas, remember to be polite, friendly, and concise. Tell them exactly who you are, why you're emailing, and what you have in mind. Don't forget to tell them what you're offering in return, too.

4. **Muster your troops.** Once you have your final list of all those who said yes, it's time to brief them. Send an email to each of your betas individually, outlining your timelines and expectations. Be clear about what you want and you'll get clear results. What I do is send all my betas an email welcoming them and thanking them for being a part of the process. I then explain what I'm expecting, such as the level of scrutiny and how they can feed their notes back to me. I always supply a copy of my book in PDF and Word file formats, asking my betas to add notes in the sidebar, or enable track changes. I then set a deadline, usually giving them between one and two months. I allow a further month for collating the feedback and making changes.

5. **Polite catch-up emails.** During the process, be sure to remember that betas are doing you a favour by editing your book. Be careful not to chase them too much. Instead send polite catch-up emails halfway through and when the deadline is drawing near,

letting your betas know you're curious to hear how they're getting on. If you haven't received feedback once the deadline passes, ask if they need more time and gently remind them of the deadline. Do chase if it's absolutely necessary.

6. **Create a dedicated folder.** When the notes and edits start to roll in, create a dedicated folder on your desktop so you can keep all the feedback in one place. It's now time to start making your changes! Use that big master list to check off which betas' notes you've gone through.

7. **Thank your betas.** And finally, be sure to thank your betas with free copies and mentions in the book or on your website. The job is done.

And that's beta-reading in a nutshell!

Cover Design

Toothpaste

Let's have a look at some toothpaste, shall we?

What do you think of the product above? Would it be something you picked up from your local supermarket shelf? Something you'd part money with? No? I thought you might say that.

If we examine this particularly drab brand of toothpaste closely, we can generate a list of what it lacks, and consequently what your book cover needs to do to impress.

First off, the toothpaste looks cheap.

If I were to slap a price on that bad boy, I'd probably say no more than 50p. In a consumer's mind, price is usually indicative of quality. That's why 99p or 99c eBooks don't actually sell that well and why I advise against setting that price point, but more on that later! A book cover as drab and as uninspiring as this toothpaste packaging will make the consumer think the book's innards are guilty of the same qualities.

You don't know what flavour it is.

From this packaging, I'd probably expect the flavour of this particular toothpaste to be something along the lines of 'month-old mushroom', or 'plain old granite'. But you have no idea what's in it. You're not told a thing. Your book cover needs to tell the prospective reader, via its design and a blurb, what it's about; or in other words, what flavour it is.

You don't want to buy it.

Your book cover's primary task is to sell itself. What this toothpaste lacks is the vital magnetic energy that makes me want to buy it. Your book cover needs to catch a reader's eye and draw them in, so that the blurb and prose can work their magic. There's a reason large companies like Nike and Apple spend a lot of moolah employing designers to work on their products and packaging, and that's to make them look attractive.

Like editing, cover design is one of the things I recommend paying for. Now we don't want to be spending piles of cash on cover design, but we do need to spend enough. Once again: you get what you pay for in this business. So spending the right amount is vital if you want to shrug off that self-publishing stigma and sell a decent number of books. There's simply no argument! A stunning, professional cover is a must. Don't use a template, or a ready-made, $5 book cover. With that in mind, why don't we have a look at a few ways of getting such a cover designed.

First of all, you need to decide what you actually want on your book cover.

Deciding what you want on your book cover

This can be tricky, especially if you're lacking a few arty bones in your body. I know I am. What helped me when creating 'The Emaneska Series' covers was putting together two mood boards for each book: one depicting the major themes of the story, the scenery of the world, and the characters; and a second one full of the best fantasy covers I could find. I set about trawling Google images and the bestseller lists on Amazon, and after a week I had a big bank of ideas and a few sketches on the backs of napkins. The result? A load of useful stuff that a designer can draw from. Pardon the pun.

Next you need to decide whether you want just an eBook format, or you want to do print as well.

Deciding which format of cover you want

The reason you need to ask yourself this question is because it will directly influence what you'll be asking your cover designer to do. Simply put, each format needs its own cover. Not a different design, but a different size and shape.

Remember that with eBooks, you won't need a back cover, primarily because eBooks don't have them! However, if you're doing print versions of your book, you will need to think about the width and design of the spine, and also what is going to be on the back cover. When these three elements are combined, they're called the cover spread: the whole book cover design that will wrap around your three-dimensional book. You will need to be able to give your designer the dimensions of the book if you want them to produce a cover spread, and this includes the spine width.

Working out the spine width for an unpublished book can be tricky while you're doing the editing, or before the formatting stage, but many print-on-demand (POD) companies have helpful size calculators and guides, working it out from the size of the book and the number of pages. This is why it's a good idea to have a firm idea of the final page count before sourcing a book cover. Fortunately, most book cover designers will understand that the spine width will change, so they'll be more than happy to go back and edit your cover spread once you have the final measurement.

Another element you need to be aware of is a barcode and your ISBN (see the section on ISBNs in **Part Two: Publish It**). You can get barcodes created pretty easily using a variety of online providers such as Lightning Source, Ingram Spark, and other companies such as Agamik. All you need to provide is your ISBN number. Barcodes should be very cheap to make, so be wary of any prices above £30/$50. Another element you need to think about is the blurb.

How to write a blurb

There is a secret art to writing a blurb. It takes a concise, commercial approach. Like the cover design itself, a blurb is designed to convince people to buy your book, to pique their interest and tickle their fancy, so to speak. The design and the blurb work in tandem as a marketing force, and this is why your blurb needs to work like a sales pitch. It needs to describe the book's content, its genre, hint at its story, and at the same time convince your potential reader that: a) your book is of a quality worth its price tag, and b) that they'll enjoy it.

Crafting the perfect blurb can take time, as you need to cram in as much intrigue and information as you can whilst keeping it short, punchy, and compelling. This can be a hard task to tackle, but if you're focused and structure your blurb well, you'll get there. Maybe look at a few examples online and emulate them. Most importantly, remember to give your blurb a thorough edit too. Your blurb is a first impression, and we all know how important they are!

Now it's just a simple matter of finding yourself a designer! Once again, we need to find ourselves a professional. Unfortunately, there are few, if any, ways of 'beta designing'. Nevertheless, I know a few ways of getting a great cover yet keeping it cheap. Let me show you:

Sourcing a book cover

DIY

This section comes with a big caveat: you should only be considering doing a DIY cover if you are a professional graphic designer. And I do mean *professional*. Day-job professional. If you can't place yourself in this category, then skip to the next paragraph. We can't afford to take any shortcuts at this point. Plenty of authors have published books with covers made in Word, covers that have been thrown together in five minutes, and they have witnessed the consequences of such DIY efforts first-hand: poor sales and bad reviews.

Now if you are a professional, you're in a lucky position. All I would recommend to you is that you try to remain objective, make sure you do your research and make yours the best damn book cover you possibly can.

Beg, borrow, and steal. Then steal some more.

For those of us who aren't graphic designers by trade, we can look to our friends, family, and colleagues instead. By exploiting (and I use that word in the nicest way possible) our existing connections, we can get professional skills at 'mates' rates'. This is what I mean by beg, borrow, and steal.

It's time to call in every favour you can and to start scouring Facebook or LinkedIn. Try to reconnect with any old friends or colleagues who might now be dabbling in design. Ask around the office, or the gym, or the coffee-shop. Who knows? That new brother-in-law of yours might turn out to be a freelance graphic artist in his spare time! Like they say:

'It's all about who you know.'

Google and recommendations

Of course, you can always use trusty old Google to find yourself a cover designer, but do be wise when you're searching – try to find freelance designers who specialise in book covers, as they will hopefully be in tune with the industry and be familiar with aspects like cover spreads and spine widths. Watch out for those package providers as well, or large design companies that lack the personal touch.

Crowd-sourcing

This is how I sourced the book cover for *The Written* and also how I found the designer for the rest of the series. As you can imagine, I recommend it quite highly!

Crowd-sourcing is an increasingly-popular way of finding designers and creating content like book covers. Crowd-sourcing works like this:

First, you post a project to a public forum that's frequented by a wide community of eager freelance creatives, semi-pros and pros alike.

These creatives then bid on your project, either with their portfolios and a quote at sites like People Per Hour or by actually having a go at your brief, like at DesignCrowd or CrowdSpring.

You can then pick and choose which design or designer you like best, commission the work, offer feedback and even complete payment through these sorts of sites.

Crowd-sourcing is very simple indeed, and it's also a great resource for things other than book covers, such as websites, t-shirt designs, graphic artists, and logos!

Here are some great crowd-sourcing sites that you can use to find designers:

- People Per Hour
- CrowdSpring
- DesignCrowd

How much should I be paying for my book cover?

That's another great question. Well, as we're on the subject of crowd-sourcing, the CrowdSpring fees are indicative of the kind of price bracket you should expect. I paid around $300 for each of my book covers (and will happily pay that again in the future) but I've also worked with designers who will do you a great book cover for under $250.

How do I make sure I get what I pay for?

Another great question! The problem is that everybody has different tastes. Some are more critical than others. Some just have an eye for design. What this means is that a cover that you might think is top-notch might not be seen in the same way by somebody else. You can trust your gut to some extent, but you also have to be brutally honest with yourself.

This is why it's important to road-test the designs that your designer comes up with. Make sure you have a panel of friends, family, fans, or fellow authors standing by to offer feedback. Make sure you compare the designs to your original brief and the images on your mood board that make your jaw go slack. Ask yourself: could you envisage your book cover next to the bestsellers of your genre, next to award-winners and big names? If the answer is a truthful yes, then you're on the right track.

Formatting

Great news – this is the final step in the polishing process! After you've edited your masterpiece and found it a stunning cover, it's time to get it ready for the publishing phase. To do that, we need to convert it into a sellable format.

What is formatting and why do we need to do it?

In a nutshell: Formatting is conversion – the conversion from one file format to another. Where books are concerned, formatting is the conversion from a word processor file, like a .doc or a .pages file, into formats that can be: a) sold as an eBook and read on eReaders, and/or b) read by a printer and come out correctly as a paperback or hardback publication.

Let's pretend we're in a bookshop for a moment, touring the gaps between the shelves. If you pick up a book and open it up, you'll see that the text fits neatly inside the margins and is well-spaced, that the chapters are well-presented and prominent, that the blank pages are cleverly arranged so that every chapter starts on the left or the right-hand side of the book. What this all means is that somebody, somewhere, has spent time resizing and rearranging the elements of a Word document into a format that looks great when printed as a 5x8 paperback.

Now let's pretend we're browsing the digital shelves of Amazon or Kobo (or Libiro!). Let's also pretend that we buy something and download it straight onto our eReader or eReading app. Once again, you'll see that the text is perfectly suited to its environment, flowing neatly over the pages with each swipe or tap. You might even see a menu option, or the ability to click on a chapter in the table of contents and fly straight to it. What this means is that somebody, somewhere, has spent time tinkering behind the scenes, adding code and links and rearranging aspects so that it fits nicely onto an eReader screen.

Now let's imagine the opposite in both cases. What if the lines were all squashed together, so the text blurred into one? What if there was little definition between the chapters? What if all the fonts were the same? Where has the table of contents gone? If you don't do your formatting right, you could be getting such comments via email – or worse: posted in the review sections on Amazon or Kobo.

Readability is very important. Secondary to editing and cover design of course, but still important. No matter how good your book is, if a reader has to buy a new pair of glasses just to be able to read your book, they're not going to be very happy. This is because readers have come to expect their books to look a certain way – the traditional way, to be frank. Decades of traditional publishing have defined what the interior of books should look like and it's wise for us indies to make sure our books fit that mould to some extent, to maximise our readers' enjoyment. Nicely separated lines, easy-to-read fonts, well-defined sections, the whole lot. And this applies to eBooks as well as print.

Formatting is also vital to your ability to make sales, especially when it comes to eBooks. If you want to sell your books all over the world, from multiple sources, then you need to format them into an industry-standard format.

Let me explain: If you're a frequent flyer, it's likely you'll have a universal plug adaptor for your laptop or hairdryer that helps you cope with all the different shapes and configurations of those odd foreign plugs. Imagine a Word file as the staunch UK three-pin plug, and an eReader as the thin nostrils of the US plug socket – there is no way they are compatible with each other. That's why you need your trusty universal plug adaptor, or to round off the analogy: why you need formatting – to be compatible with the industry and therefore to be able to sell your books at stores like Amazon, stores that are file format-specific.

So this is formatting – not just the process of making your book look like a book but also a conversion to an industry-compatible format. Onwards then!

The extra bits

But wait! Before you format there are a few things to add to your masterpiece if you haven't already. The following aspects are common, but may have escaped your attention up until now.

The copyright page

This is normally the first page that readers see. To speak frankly again, it is largely ignored, but it is essential for asserting your copyright and ownership of the work. Here's a rough example of a standard copyright page that you can use:

Copyright © [**Insert author or publisher name here**] 20XX

The right of [**Insert author name here**] to be identified as the author of this work has been asserted by [**him/her**] in accordance with the Copyright, Designs and Patents Act 1988 (or other similar law, depending on your country). All rights reserved.

No part of this book may be reproduced, stored in a retrieval system, or transmitted, in any form, or by any means (electronic, mechanical, photocopying, recording or otherwise) without the prior written permission of the [**author/publisher**], except in cases of brief quotations embodied in reviews or articles. It may not be edited, amended, lent, resold, hired out, distributed or otherwise circulated without the publisher's written permission.

Permission can be obtained from **[Insert contact email or website here]**

[All characters in this book are fictitious and any resemblance to real persons, living or dead, is purely coincidental.]

[Insert your own book identifier code if needed]
[ISBN: XXX-X-XXXXXXX-X-X]
[Insert edition and format here – define eBook if an eBook version]
[Published by XXXX in 20XX]
[Cover design by XXXX]
[Edited by XXXX]
[Cover photo © XXXX 20XX]
[Printed by XXXX]

Every section in a bold bracket needs input, whereas every section in italics is optional. What you include depends on how you publish your books, what you publish and who you want to reference. The important parts are the permissions and the assertion of your copyright at the beginning.

Do bear in mind that you'll need different copyright pages for your digital and print versions – detailing what format each edition takes.

The title page

This is a simple page that states the title and the author of the book. For eBooks, particularly Kindle books, it is sometimes found in front of the copyright page, almost as a simple book cover. Here's an example:

I, INDIE

Book One of the Rest

By

Anne Author

The 'About the author' page

I would class this as a prerequisite for any book. It's your chance to put a face to a name, to market yourself or your persona, and to tell the reader exactly who and what you are. This is great if you're a non-fiction writer, as it's a chance to share any academic accolades you might have earned and to tell the reader exactly why you're qualified to write your book. If you're a fiction writer, you can do the same by listing any previous works or accomplishments in the world of books. It's also a chance to share links to your website and social media, ensuring that your readers can find you if they like your book and want to connect.

The table of contents

This is a must for non-fiction titles, but optional for fiction. For instance, my fantasy books don't have a table of contents, or 'ToC', but this book does. It's a personal decision based on the type of content in your book. If you do want to include a ToC, make sure you make it easy to understand and include the page numbers so that readers can easily navigate the book.

A quick note on: *eBooks and ToCs*

Almost all eBooks, both fiction and non-fiction, will have a ToC. This is because with eBooks you can't just fold over a page or slip in a bookmark so that you can carry on from where you left off, or simply flip to a page number without scrolling madly with your fingers. Although some eReaders and apps feature a bookmark function, readers are still largely dependent on being able to dart back and forth through a book. This is why a ToC is vital for eBooks. It's part of their code. It may sound like a headache, but fortunately for us authors, a

ToC can be created by your formatter during the eBook formatting process.

If you would like to create your own ToC while you are working on your book, you can do this in Word by highlighting chapter or section names, going to Insert, and clicking 'Insert Bookmark'. Once you've named your bookmark, you can go back to your ToC, highlight the relevant section names and then convert them into hyperlinks. These hyperlinks can be the bookmarks that you've just assigned. Hey presto, you have a ToC that can help you dart back and forth through your book!

The dedication

This is another optional extra, but one that gives your book a personal touch. As you might already know, authors frequently dedicate books to those who have inspired or helped them along the way. Personally, I'm always very intrigued by dedications. It's nice to wonder who these people are, and how they may have helped the author. This is also a great place to thank your beta readers!

The acknowledgments

The acknowledgements normally come at the back of the book, and in a way, are extensions of the dedication. It's a chance to publicly thank any other people who didn't make the cut for the dedication and also to show off a bit more of your personality. It's also a great place to thank your editor.

The extra, extra bits

The inclusion of any other extras depends on the type of book you've written. For instance, non-fiction books might need bibliographies, glossaries, or references. Personally, I like to put a little cross-selling marketing into my books. By this I simply mean putting adverts for the eBook version in the paperback version and vice versa. It can help to boost sales of both formats – something that's called cross-selling. I also like to include a little sneak peek of my next book, if I can. This is important if you want to keep readers hooked and excited for your next book. Combining these with website and social media links can really help when you're trying to build a fan base. The options are endless! It's your book, so you can do what you like with it. Just make sure it doesn't spoil or detract from the reading experience, as that's the most important aspect of all.

Now, because books can now be both print and digital, there are consequently two different types of formatting:

formatting for eBooks and formatting for print, which includes paperbacks and hardbacks. I want to discuss print first.

Print formatting

Often referred to as typesetting, print formatting is a little less technical, or rather *digital*, than eBook formatting, so it's a good starting point and will help you get into the formatting frame of mind.

The first thing to understand about typesetting is that, like editing and cover design, there are professionals out there who can do it for you and make a damn good job of it too. My advice, as always, is to use a professional to attain the high quality you need to succeed. However, it is a skill that can be learnt. I now typeset all my own books, as I spent time learning how to do it and practising into the early hours of various mornings. Learning how to typeset and format can save you money, but you will always run the risk of not being as good as a professional. Just remember to stay objective, to keep practising and to have a pro standing by, just in case.

The objective of print formatting is to convert your word processor document into a PDF format – a common format that is used by most print-on-demand printers. What they need is a PDF version of your book that exhibits the exact same layout and dimensions as a paperback or hardback book. They don't make any changes or amendments, they simply print the PDF directly. This is why it has to be perfect.

The print PDF itself isn't all that hard to make – most word processors can generate PDF versions of documents very easily. What is somewhat tricky is manhandling all the elements of your manuscript, such as chapter names and page numbers, into something that resembles a published book. It's tricky, but it actually doesn't involve as much skill as editing or cover design. All you need is a good eye for layout, a bit of word processor know-how, and patience. Here are my ten easy steps you can follow to learn how to format for print.

1. **Look at other books in your genre.** Wander into your nearest bookshop and note how the interior of books should look. This will give you an idea of what your book needs to look like, and hopefully give you a few clever ideas in the process.

2. **Save yourself a copy.** When you're ready to start formatting, save your book as a new copy, so that if you make a mistake, you're only affecting the new copy, not your original manuscript.

3. **Change the page size.** Word processor documents tend to use a default A4 size, so if you haven't already, you'll need to change the page size to that of a book. You should have already decided on the size of your book when sourcing the cover, so just apply that size to your document. Industry-standard book

sizes are normally supplied by your chosen POD printer.

4. **Page numbers and headers.** Add the page numbers and headers, keeping them in line with what you've learnt from other books.

5. **Line or text spacing.** Widen the line or text spacing. This makes for easier reading. A spacing of 1.2–1.4 should be enough.

6. **Set the margins.** By dragging the horizontal and vertical margins of your page in and out, you can make sure that no text is lost in the depths of the spine when the book is bound together and that the words are not too close to the outside edge.

7. **Set the overall font size.** 11pt is always a good size, as this ensures you don't add too many pages to your book while the print stays readable at the same time.

8. **Layout.** Then go through your book, page by page, and make the layout sing. This is where you add any blank pages and page breaks, decide on chapter heading fonts and sizes, and bring together the general layout. Be creative if you like, but make sure you keep it professional!

9. **Check, check, and check again.** Consistency is the key here. If you add a page at the start of the book, remember that it might push all subsequent pages

along. This is why you need to check over and over again that the layout is consistent and just the way you want it. I always make notes on font size and use the find and replace function to quickly skip through my book during final checks.

10. **Export!** And once you are absolutely, unequivocally, irrefutably happy with your layout, and confident that it's right, it's time to export it as a PDF document, ready to upload!

And that's my quick guide to typesetting! Once again, as long as you remember to stay consistent and aim for the loftiest heights of professionalism and quality, then you'll be fine. If at any point you feel it's not good enough, for any reason, then it's time to redo it or source a professional.

eBook formatting

This is a bit of a different game, and here's the reason why: **eBooks are a little bit like mobile apps**. They might have the same content, but they look different on different devices. Some may even behave differently. Functions that exist on one device might not exist on another. The reason for this is that different screen sizes and operating systems affect how an app looks and how it runs.

The same is true of eBooks. Being of digital matter, they behave a bit like apps. A copy of *The Written* on my Kobo reading app behaves differently to how it might on my Readmill app. The content is the same, but the way the app or device presents it is different. As such, eBook formatting requires a certain level of knowledge of digital trickery – things like coding and device behaviour.

This is why I always outsource my eBook formatting. I used to do it myself, and could get a book to work quite well on various eReaders, but the world of digital reading moves faster than a cheetah at a buffet. Thanks to the new generations of eReaders that have enhanced functionality, formatting is now more complicated than it used to be. eBook formatting is now more akin to website coding than it is to print formatting.

So where do we find eBook formatters? It can be tricky, as they're not as common as editors and cover designers. Once again, reach out to your author communities to find freelancers or affordable, reputable companies. Google can also help to a certain extent. Don't forget – it's also a service that I can offer through Shelf Help.

When getting your eBooks formatted, bear in mind that there are different types of eBook. There are three main file formats that you will need to convert your manuscript into. Each has their own different set of rules (which is another reason I outsource eBook formatting!) and compatible eReaders. Now, this may all sound rather confusing, but it's actually quite simple: Amazon and Kindles use the **.mobi** format, which has some restrictions on font style and embedded images. The rest of the major stores and eReaders (such as Kobo and B&N) use the popular **ePub** format, which can feature more media and is more customisable. Lastly, there's Adobe's PDF format, which isn't a dedicated eBook format, but is used more for PC and mobile reading, especially in developing markets.

My advice is to have your eBook formatter create all three formats if possible. (You may be able to create PDFs yourself using some word processors.) This ensures you can be available from all stores, on all eReading platforms, to all readers. There is definite merit in being available on all stores – it simply increases your chances of being discovered. There's no better way to put it, and that's why I always advise avoiding exclusivity and going for maximum availability instead.

Lastly, don't forget to get your formatter to attach your **metadata** in your eBook. This is the information that is digitally bonded to your book file. Metadata includes the title, author and ISBN, but most importantly, **keywords or tags**. Some of you may already be familiar with tags and keywords. They can also be assigned during the ePublishing stage and help you pop up when readers search for certain words at stores. (We'll be getting to ePublishing shortly!)

Basically, **keywords and tags** are descriptive words that relate directly to your book, its genre, its style and anything else you can think of that will bring new readers straight to you. For instance, for 'The Emaneska Series' I would use keywords like 'dark fantasy', or 'epic battles'.

Keywords do require a bit of thought, however, so make sure you test keywords with tools like Google's Keyword Planner, which is part of Adwords. (Just make sure you don't accidentally start a pay-per-click campaign – they can lead straight to bankruptcy if you're not careful!) Also, be aware that if you want to change your keywords at any point, you'll probably have to ask your formatter to produce a new eBook, and then republish it. That's why it's wise to get them right on the first go, if you can.

So in summary...

It looks like it's time to strike a big line through the **Polish It** section – we're done! By the end of this stage, you should have an attractive, professional-looking product sitting pretty on your hard drive. If you're anything like me at this stage, you'll likely be itching to get publishing and selling. Let's recap what we've learnt:

● **Three stages.** The process of polishing your book is one of three stages: editing, cover design and formatting.

● **Use professionals to attain success.** It's important to hire professionals where possible to help you attain the standards necessary for success.

● **Editor or beta readers.** Where editing is concerned, you can use a freelance pro editor, or use the cheaper method of beta reading.

● **Second draft.** It's important to do a second draft before you approach any editors and also to spend time finding the right sort of editor for you.

● **Careful beta planning.** Beta readers should also be carefully chosen and the beta-reading process carefully structured to ensure you get the best feedback possible.

- **Professional cover design.** Cover design, in 99.9% of all cases, will require a professional designer to help you get that stunning cover your book deserves.

- **Brilliant yet affordable.** There are many ways of finding cover designers, but it's important to make sure you find the best, and one that's affordable. This is why you should always try calling in any favours first from friends, family, and contacts, if you can.

- **Dimensions and editions.** Don't forget to decide on the dimensions, width, and whether you want to do print as well as eBook editions before approaching a designer. This means you won't waste their time, and that you can get the right sort of cover designs for the publishing stage.

- **Formatting.** Formatting for print is easier than eBook formatting, as the latter requires more technical know-how. It can be learnt, but you need to spend time and effort getting it right, and drawing inspiration from traditionally published books.

- **Pros and plural formats.** Once again, you'll likely need a professional individual or company to format your eBooks. You'll also need two or three formats: **.ePub** (if you're going to sell books at stores other than Amazon), **.mobi** (if you want to sell on Amazon) and **PDF** (if needed).

- **Metadata and ISBNs.** Don't forget to think about your metadata at this stage. Doing it now will help you be consistent when you come to publish. Also getting print and eBook **ISBNs** at this stage might save you a little bit of time when you come to the publishing stage. Jump to the paragraph on 'What to think about before you think about publishing' in the **Publish It** section, which begins just overleaf!

Now it's time for that all-important stage – becoming a published author.

Part 2 | *Publish It*

What to think about before you think about publishing

To quote a very archaic phrase:

'There are many ways to skin a cat.'

What you might want, or what might suit you, may not be another author's cup of tea. Simply put, every author is different and that's why it's hard just to say: 'Here is how you publish. End of story.'

The truth is that the indie and digital revolution have given us choices. There are now many different paths to publishing your books and each author will have their preferred way. This depends on your goals, books, genre, skills and a whole host of other aspects. Only one thing matters and that is **what is best for you and your career**. What this section will do is introduce you to the spectrum of publishing options within the Shelf Help method. That way you can make an informed decision and hopefully say to yourself: 'Yes! That's the one for me.'

If at any point you're feeling lost and drowned by the number of options, just remember to focus on what it is you want. What is your end goal? Do you want to get your book in bookstores? Do you only want to publish eBooks? Do you want to be exclusive to Amazon? These are the questions you need to ask yourself. First, set your goals. Second, find out how to achieve them. We'll be discussing the various methods of publishing in this section so by the end of it, you'll be able to assess your goals and make your decision!

There are also a few bits and pieces we need to chat about first, before we leap into publishing our books. Some of you might be familiar with things like ISBNs, metadata and prices, but for those of you who aren't, I'm going to break down the jargon for you.

ISBNs

An **ISBN**, or International Standard Book Number, is a unique identifier for your book. An ISBN enables you to be searchable in stores and via the internet. Bookshops also use them when ordering books from distributors. They're essentially an industry-standard, so you really do want to use them. Don't forget that if you're publishing in print, you'll also need a barcode for your back cover. (See the section about what you need on your book cover in **Part One: Polish It**.)

ISBN 978-0-9567700-1-1

This is a barcode.
(Note the corresponding ISBN at the top.)

I always recommend getting your own ISBNs as it means you'll own them and be registered as the publisher, which I believe is very important – just think back to the story about Vantage Press. If you buy or use an ISBN from places like Smashwords or package providers, they will be registered as the owner. (Although, for the small fee of $15, Smashwords can provide you with an ISBN that does have you registered as the publisher.) Now why would you want somebody else listed on your ISBN when you're the one doing all the hard work? This is why I always advise buying ISBNs directly from ISBN agencies, such as Bowker (US) or Nielsen (UK).

If you're going to publish multiple formats or editions of your book, such as a paperback and an .ePub, then you'll need two ISBNs – a print ISBN and an eISBN – one for each. There's no real difference between these two, except for the editions they're assigned to. Agencies just stipulate that there has to be a different ISBN for each format. It's so they can avoid confusion, more than anything. Some of you might be wondering about your .mobi file and your Amazon edition at this point. Well, the good news is that Amazon don't require you to have an ISBN – they give you an ASIN instead, which is essentially their own version. Nice and simple!

Metadata

Simply speaking, **metadata** is the information attached to your book, your ISBN and/or embedded into its file (as we discussed in the eBook formatting section). Metadata is made up of many different little elements: title, blurb, keywords, categories, dimensions, weight, page count, author name, publisher name, ISBNs... the lot. Metadata includes every bit of data surrounding your book. It's wise to gather and note down all the metadata you can before you publish, so you know your book will be consistently represented across the board.

Now, I mentioned that metadata can be attached to your ISBN, but I also said that ISBNs are an element of metadata in their own right. This may sound confusing, so let me explain. When you purchase an ISBN from an agency, they will want to know all sorts of information for their database. As such, they may request certain details such as book title, edition, author name, price and subject codes. This data – metadata – is now attached to your ISBN. When a bookshop uses the ISBN to search for your book, their database, which is connected to the agency's, returns all that data. This is another reason why we need to use ISBNs, so that all our information is searchable too. They are useful little things.

The way that ISBN information is used is what makes the difference. Some companies, such as Amazon or Kobo, treat an ISBN as simply another piece of data and rely on author input. Other companies will actually use the metadata from the ISBN database. This means that when we buy our ISBNs, we need to provide the exact same data we'd give to Amazon when publishing to the Kindle store. Don't just assume the ISBN metadata won't be seen because it will, normally in stores that don't provide direct access to authors.

So if you didn't prepare your metadata earlier, you may need some of following:

- Book title
- Author name
- Publisher name (if different)
- A blurb
- Publication date
- ISBN
- Edition number
- Format (such as paperback or .ePub)
- Height and width/trim size (for print books)Weight
- Binding type

- List price/RRP (make sure to expect multiple currencies)
- Keywords/tags (either embedded into your eBook file or selected when publishing)
- Age/literacy rating (not a common one, usually asked for when setting up the ISBN itself)
- Categories/Subject (the industry standard is the BISAC subject headings list, which will give you a head start for when you come to publish or buy your ISBNs)

Prices

It may sound like a simple subject, but a lot of thought needs to go into the pricing of your books. Too high, and they may not sell. Too low, and customers might assume they're low quality. And of course, where print books are concerned, there are unit costs and wholesale discounts to be aware of. We'll discuss those in greater depth in the print publishing section.

To get a good price for your books you'll need to do a spot of research first. Head to the online bookstores and find some books that are similar to yours, both self-published and traditional. They need to be similar in respect to genre but also in word count, or in other words – size. Make a note of their prices and how well they appear to be selling. This will give you some indication of the area you should be aiming for.

Now don't forget, if we want to be global authors, we have to figure out prices for multiple currencies and markets. You can use a currency converter, but just remember that straight conversions don't often translate very well. For instance, Take the epic fantasy best-seller *A Game of Thrones*. You can buy *GoT* in paperback in Australia for the discounted price of 17.99 AUD. Using my handy currency converter, that gives me a price of 16.35 USD (as of December 2013). But wait, the same paperback on Amazon.com (again, as of December 2013) is priced at 13.44 USD. The Mass Market paperback is even cheaper: 8.22 USD. Back in Australian dollars, that's a pinch over nine dollars. See what I mean? Prices aren't always directly interchangeable.

Pricing can also be a little bit of a game, especially when it comes to eBooks. Thanks to the ease of ePublishing, we can shuffle our pricing around almost daily, following trends or being competitive. Just make sure you don't do anything too drastic!

So to understand how we can publish our books, we'll need to look at the industry again, and how the cogs of its machine interact with each other. Let's start with print publishing first.

Print Publishing

Many of today's indie authors sadly dismiss print, believing it to be too difficult, too expensive, or simply not worth the effort. Well, I'm here to say that's all rubbish. Once again, technology has come to the rescue, and today's indie author has access to a range of digital, high-quality, agile and affordable printing solutions, many of which come with incredible distribution connections and access to major bookshops. To understand how they work, let's look at how the physical world works.

The journey from the printing press to the readers' hands

Via the medium of the illustrious flow chart, I've outlined the three main print publishing processes that exist today – one is used by the traditional publishing industry and the other two are processes commonly used by us indies.

The traditional model

Publisher publishes book
(Books usually printed en masse)

Books shipped to
distributors

– Bookshops
– Distributor

Distributor ships books to
bookshops or online stores

Returns and damages are
handled by the distributor,
feeding back to the publisher.

Bookshops and stores
sell books to
customers

The indie model: POD

Books published via a POD printer
Made available in catalogues, stores
and bookshop databases

Customer orders book
at a bookshop or
online store

– Author
– POD printer
– Bookshop
– Distributor

The book is then
printed to order

If the book is selling well, the
bookstore can then buy more
copies direct from the
distributor

It is then shipped to the
customer or the bookstore
via a distributor

The indie model: Bulk printing

Books printed in bulk. either a 'short run' or a 'long run'

Books are then shipped to the author for storage

If author has struck a deal with a bookshop or distributor, books can be shipped straight to them

Author sells books to family and friends, at events, or to local bookshops

Distributor makes the books available to major stores. Ships books when ordered.

$

- Author
- Printer
- Bookshop
- Distributor

After looking at these diagrams, bells might already be ringing. You might already have an inkling of which model suits you, your books and also your skill-set. But wait! Knowledge is power, so they say, so let's quickly discuss the mathematics behind print books.

Unit costs, RRPs and wholesale discounts

The number one thing to remember about any print company, and any relationship with a distributor, is that they will undoubtedly want a slice of your profit pie. What you need to understand is why each slice is taken and how big it is. This is important because it will help you understand how big *your* slice will be. If it's a minuscule sliver, either cut out some of the middle men if you can, or find a cheaper printer.

One term you will come across at printers like Lightning Source and CreateSpace is **wholesale discount**. This is the customary discount that you give to distributors and bookshops, so that when they sell your books on to customers at the **list price** (otherwise known as the **recommended retail price**, or **RRP**) they can make a profit. The industry standard for wholesale discount, traditionally speaking, is around 50-55% (in the UK, that is. In other countries it can range from 40%-60%). This is a big slice, and if there are one or two distributors in between you and the reader, either your profit is going to be low, or your list price will have to be higher than average. Neither of these options is ideal for indies.

While Lightning Source allows us to set our own wholesale discount, CreateSpace does not. It's set at 40% of the list price, which isn't too bad. However, if you're interested in that Expanded Distribution service, be aware that any book sold through an Expanded channel means a discount of 60%. So, a wider reach, but a bigger bite out of your pie.

Here's an example of how it all works, using POD provider **Lightning Source**:

I've written a 300 page book. Lightning Source will charge me £3.70 per unit to print it. I set the list price at £8.99, not a bad price for a paperback in the UK. This leaves a slice of £5.29. Let's say I then decide to use Lightning's distribution connections with Gardners, so that I can sell my books in chains like Waterstones. In an effort to meet industry standards I set my wholesale discount at 50%, which means Gardners buys my book at £4.50. So what do I make, on each book sold? About 80p. Under 10%. Not very inspiring at all is it?

But let's say I reduce my wholesale discount to 35%, a 'short discount' as it's called in the trade. Gardners now buys my book in at £5.84. This gives me a slightly fatter slice of £2.14, a veritable dream for most traditional authors! The remaining £3.15 is then split between Gardners and Waterstones.

But wait: Waterstones, being the last link in the chain, normally has to take what Gardners leaves behind. As

Gardners is storing, shipping, and delivering these books, you can imagine it will probably take the lion's share of that £3.15. This doesn't leave much for Waterstones. Depending on how large its slice is, Gardners may not be willing to buy your books in because the profit margin will be so low. It simply won't be worth the company's time.

Of course, you can afford to give away a higher discount if your unit cost is lower. This is where printing in bulk can be useful. We'll come onto that shortly.

It's all about balance and whether you want control over your discounting. As we just discussed in the pricing section, please don't just slap a number on your book, like some authors do, and hope for the best. You need to be aware of exactly where all the slices of your pie go. It will help you work out what level of discounting is acceptable, your profit margin, your RRP or last price, and ultimately, which printer you want to use.

A quick note on: *making changes*

Even though Shelf Help promotes a technology-driven approach, some technology has its limits. We live in the physical world and although we can access our book digitally, sometimes making changes can cost money, as changes mean making physical changes to the original document. For instance, if you spot a typo in your book and want it changed, changing your file with a POD printer or reprinting books with a short run printer will cost money. It's important to bear this in mind, especially during the editing stage, or when you're planning a new edition. It isn't like ePublishing, where changes are normally free and fast too. Changes to print books can take a little longer.

POD Printing

POD is a very popular option for today's indie. Thank to its digital nature it's agile, it means you don't have to hold any stock, and some of the best POD printers can produce books that are almost indistinguishable from those printed in bulk. The self-publishing boom has given birth to some great POD companies. In this section I want to look at two of the biggest, best, and most highly recommended by myself and other authors: **CreateSpace** and **Lightning Source**.

Lightning Source

Now that self-publishing has come of age, we have some great options available to us. Companies that previously served only publishers have opened their gates wide to indie authors. Lightning Source is one of these companies. What's important to know about Lightning Source is that it isn't a standalone company – it is operated by the **world's largest book distributor**, Ingram. What does this mean? Well, we've already seen how integral distributors are to the print market. With Lightning Source, you're not just handling the printing, you're ticking the distribution box as well. And what a distribution channel it is! Ingram is a global distribution network, one that has printing locations on several continents (such as North America, two European locations, and also Australia), affiliations with all major bookshops and access to other distributors like Gardners and Bertrams. What you're getting for your money here isn't just printing, it's access – access to the same network as the big five publishers. A level playing field, anyone?

Lightning Source is reasonably simple and straightforward. They don't offer any other services besides printing and distribution, eBook distribution, and the ability to make you a barcode. You simply apply for an account with them, fill out a few forms and then you're allocated a dashboard. From this dashboard, you have the ability to view reports, order books, make changes, and of course, publish titles. That's the beauty of having such a digital backbone to this self-publishing revolution. This is why I always promote a technology-driven approach. It's just so convenient and centralised.

When publishing a title, all Lightning Source need from you is an edited and formatted PDF, a PDF of your cover spread, your ISBN and all the book data we discussed earlier, such as pricing and description. You'll also need to know what type and size of book you want, the prices, and what level of wholesale discount you want to give away. Lightning

Source, like most POD printers, will have a range of trim sizes, paper-types, and finishes available. You simply choose what you want from their list.

The costs of publishing with Lightning Source come from both the unit cost and the actual fee for setting up a new title. Neither are expensive, relatively speaking. The title set-up fee remains the same – £42/$75 – for both your book file and cover file (for both black & white books and colour!). Unit costs are based on a flat fee depending on the size and type of your book, and then a per-page cost. The flat fee is £0.70/$0.90, the per-page cost is £0.01/$0.013. This means that a 300-page book (measuring 5x8 inches) will cost £3.70/$4.80. This is the cost per unit, which is deducted from your compensation, or in other words, your sales. Don't worry, you don't have to pay it. It's automatically deducted, therefore a cost, but not a direct one.

Other costs include proof copies and of course, making changes. You can get proof copies before you agree to your book's publication, at £10/$15 for a paperback and £13/$20 for a hardback (+£0.07/$0.09 per page). Don't forget, changes will cost here. Lightning Source charges £45/$40 per half an hour for working on changes.

Lightning Source has been around a long time, and although it was originally launched in 1997 to provide POD services to publishers, you wouldn't notice. It feels like it's designed for indies. They pay monthly and their print costs are very affordable – something that's very important in the POD world. Lightning Source's quality is also second to none, as far as POD printing goes, and they offer a wide range of book sizes, formats, paper types, and finishes. I use Lightning Source exclusively for all my print books (hardbacks as well!) and I can safely say they look and feel every bit as good as a traditional book.

Lightning Source also has a sister company called **Ingram Spark**. Like Lightning Source, Spark also offers authors a dashboard and its abilities and requirements are largely the same. While you can publish eBooks using Lightning Source (that's right, Ingram has a digital catalogue too!) it's not the most intuitive process, and that's where Spark comes in. It's refined that process so that you can publish both formats at the same time, to the wide network that is Ingram. Like Lightning Source, Spark feels as though it was designed specifically for indies, though it has a smarter-looking dashboard. The only drawback with Spark is that authors cannot set their own wholesale discount (which is set at 40% – not too bad all things considered). This can be quite an issue when it comes to unit costs, so for me Lightning Source wins by a nose. But of course, the choice is up to you. As long as you investigate both, you'll be able to make a smart decision.

CreateSpace

Now we've looked at what you get when a distributor offers POD services, let's look at what you get when a major retailer wades into POD waters.

What makes CreateSpace unique is that it's owned and run by Amazon. Just as Lightning Source's POD offering is linked with their parent distribution network, CreateSpace's offering is linked to the **biggest online store on the planet**: Amazon.

First launched in 2009, CreateSpace offers authors the chance to publish a variety of different types of books and to have them distributed direct to the Amazon store from Amazon's very own warehouses. What this means is that compared to Lightning Source, you're one step closer to the reader (those who are Amazon users, that is). This can mean faster delivery times and direct control over what metadata appears alongside your book in the store.

Like Lightning Source, the unit costs of printing your book are made up of a flat fee and a per-page fee. The fixed charges vary slightly depending on which location or store your book is printed or sold at. For Amazon.com, the CreateSpace eStore (a dedicated store for all the books published by CreateSpace) and books with Expanded Distribution (see below), a 300-page book (once again 5x8) would cost $0.85 per book and $0.012 per page. This cost jumps a bit if you're printing a book with less than 108 pages, to $2.15. For books printed and sold in the UK it's £0.70 per book and £0.01 per page.

However, what Amazon doesn't quite have is the distribution network that Ingram has. CreateSpace does offer the Expanded Distribution service (which is actually free) which does give authors access to most of the Ingram network, but it's limited outside the United States.

Another issue is that CreateSpace authors in the UK who want to order books for themselves unfortunately have to order them from Amazon's US printing location, and therefore pay a larger shipping fee. This means that your unit cost goes up and your profit goes down. In my eyes, this is quite a drawback to me as I sell a lot of books at events and to friends, but this might not affect you. Once again, it's a personal choice of how you want to play the game.

Like Lightning Source, there's a big range of printing options available when it comes to binding types, sizes, and finishes. CreateSpace does offer a hardback option, but it isn't one of their main offerings and is only available to the author to buy. However, hardbacks aren't often the priority for many indie authors. Personally, I offer both paperback *and* hardback versions of my books, as many fantasy readers are keen to get their hands on a premium edition. Releasing another format can provide an additional revenue stream, but you need to weigh up the time and effort it will take against how well you think hardbacks will sell in your genre and market.

CreateSpace also provides authors with other services such as cover design, editing, formatting and marketing. Now, you might be thinking that this sounds like one of those package providers we were talking about earlier, but no. Let me assure you, Amazon are very reputable indeed, and their services are completely optional and reasonably priced. Do have a little look at the services, especially when considering your polishing options!

Bulk printing

Although it is important to discuss this option, in my opinion, printing in bulk doesn't quite sit within the realm of the Shelf Help method. It is a process that is too reminiscent of the days of vanity presses for my liking. To me, what it embodies is a large initial investment and a very manual process for making your money back. Selling 3000 or 2000, or even 1000 print books by hand to friends, family, bookshops, and readers is a very hard thing to pull off, especially when you haven't got any major distribution connections. And don't forget, we're not just talking about the initial cost of printing here; you have to factor in the storage, shipping and selling costs as well. Essentially, you run the risk of never breaking even or making profit. To me, as an author-preneur, that's not a risk I'd like to take!

But printing in bulk isn't all bad, not by any stretch of the imagination. The good thing about bulk printing is that unit costs are usually much lower than a POD book. The POD unit cost for a 300-page book, as we've seen, can be around £3-£4/$4-$5, where unit costs for bulk printing can be up to 50% less, depending on the volume you need.

The quality of a bulk-printed book can often be better too. Although the digital presses of Lightning Source and CreateSpace can produce books near-indistinguishable from traditionally-printed books, the offset lithographic printing methods used by most bulk printers (some do use very advanced digital presses) mean that you're not compromising for a cheaper unit cost. Offset lithography printing ensures both high, commercial quality as well as a low cost. Printing runs of books at the same time can also mean a higher level of consistency across the board, as well as greater flexibility in materials, sizes, binding types, and finishes.

The truth is that authors can do and are doing clever things by printing titles in bulk. If you want to avoid the cost of selling books by hand, it's possible to set up agreements with distributors and wholesalers so that your book can be made available to all major bookshops. Gardners, for instance, offer a small publisher service where you can ship large orders directly to their warehouses for distribution to all major UK bookshops. You can do something very similar with Amazon too, with their Advantage and Marketplace programmes. However, selling your books this way might entail large initial investments, storage or warehousing fees, and taking care of fine details such as sales, stock and returns. It's that fine balance between control and workload. Once again, it's down to you, the author!

We can also look at short run printing. I'm not talking thousands and thousands of copies here, I'm talking runs of 100-500 books. Short runs decrease the initial investment, and therefore the risk, whilst keeping quality high.

For example, you could publish a special edition of your book for a particular event, perhaps. Or why not create a very premium and limited edition and sell it direct from your site. You could even use POD and bulk in tandem if you need to, using POD for selling at a distance, and then print a short run for signings and/or selling directly to local bookshops. It's all about being clever and exploiting the advantages of both types of printing without getting bogged down by the manual processes. Bulk printing is a different string to your bow, but a string nonetheless.

How to find a bulk printer

Bulk printers may by easy to find, but finding the *right* printer takes a little more effort. Again, it's a personal decision. The good news is that there are many different types of bulk printers out there – ranging from lithographic, to offset, to digital presses. Not only that, but our two major POD printers Lightning Source and CreateSpace also offer bulk printing options, as well as their core POD services. I would highly recommend looking to them if you are already printing your books on demand, and want to try short run.

If you do want to look at larger print runs, or offset and lithographic printing, then my advice would be to get Googling. This may sound a little untrustworthy, but as we authors and our needs are so varied, it would be hard for me to be unwavering in any recommendations. This is why it's important to do your own research and find the right printer for you and your books. However, I do have some recommendations for reliable and well-known printers, which you can find at the end of this section.

When you think you've found a printer that tickles your fancy, make sure you investigate and evaluate them thoroughly. You should be asking the following sorts of questions:

- What are their unit costs?
- Are they cheaper or more expensive than others?
- What finishes, materials, trim sizes and binding types do they offer?
- What is their print quality like?
- Can you see a sample?
- What are their delivery/shipping costs?
- Would a printer in the local area be cheaper?
- What are their turnaround times?
- What are their delivery times?
- Do they ship abroad?
- What are their packing costs?
- Do they handle orders or do any distribution?
- What do you need to provide to them?

By creating a short list of likely printers, you can then assess them one by one, giving them scores based on the questions above. Only then can you make a data-driven decision, and choose the printer that suits you to a tee.

There's a good chance you'll come across printers that also offer other publishing services, such as eBook formatting or a little cover design on the side. By all means take a look at these services. Who knows? They might be cheaper and/or better than some of your alternatives. There's never any harm in taking a look around and investigating options, but remember to keep an eye out for the sort of providers we talked about at the beginning of this guide – those that package together services and charge a fortune for them. The rule of thumb here is to always be wary of any multi-service offering. When coming across a provider, always dig into their terms and conditions, cast an eye over their prices and be mindful of their quality. You really don't want to fall foul of these sorts of companies and I'm sure if you keep your wits about you, you won't.

And that's printing in bulk!

So in summary...

Print publishing is an aspect of being an indie that is often deemed either too difficult or not worth the time and effort, but I hope we've proved both these assumptions wrong in this section. Before we turn our attention to the world of digital and to the glorious eBook, let's recap:

- **Do your sums.** When producing print books you need to be aware of unit costs, RRPs, and wholesale discounts. The unit cost is what a book costs to print. This may be comprised of a fixed fee and then a per-page charge when working with a POD printer, or a simple print cost when printing in bulk. The list price, or recommended retail price (RRP), is the price you set for the consumer. The wholesale discount is the discount on the list price that you give to those in between the printer and the consumer. In the traditional world this is set at a standard 50-55% (in the UK, that is. In other countries in can range from 40%-60%), but with some POD printers like Lightning Source, you can set your own discount, meaning a larger royalty for you. This is called short discounting, and is typically around 35-435%. Just bear in mind what it means for the store and the distributor, who are having their shares down-sized.

- **Don't forget the little things.** Before you can think about publishing your books in print, you'll need to take care of a few remaining aspects and make a few decisions. These take the form of ISBNs, metadata, and pricing.

- **ISBNs** are a necessity in the land of print. You will need one ISBN per edition or format and can buy them from ISBN agencies Bowker (US) and Nielsen (UK). By buying them yourself, it means that you – not another publishing company – are the registered owner.

- **Metadata** can be attached to your ISBN, attached to your eBook file, or entered into the publishing dashboards of POD printers, eBook stores and distributors. This is a good time to get all your metadata together and compile it into one master document. Metadata is comprised of many different elements, such as ISBNS, genres, categories, dimensions, prices, descriptions and keywords. Compiling it now helps you publish swiftly and correctly, as you'll know what you want ahead of time and have it to hand when you need it. It will also help you to stay consistent throughout the process of publishing.

- **Pricing** is an important aspect and therefore needs a lot of thought. Do some research into the market so you can get an idea of the price of books that are similar to yours in both genre and length. When deciding on prices in other currencies, remember to check stores in other countries to see what the average price of books is. Don't just use a straight currency conversion.

- **Size matters.** To be ready for print publishing, your book needs to be formatted for the specific print size you've chosen, and available in a high-quality PDF format.

- **There are different types of print publishing.** Indies have two choices when it comes to print publishing: using a POD (print-on-demand) printer, or to print in bulk.

- **Agility**. POD printing is an agile way of getting books onto both digital and physical shelves. With POD, books are simply printed and shipped to order, requiring almost zero involvement from you except for an upload, some data entry and a small publishing fee.

- **Affordable and global.** POD printing means a lower initial investment and, if you use the right printers, access to global book distributors like Ingram and Gardners – the same ones as the traditional publishers use.

- **Quality is always paramount.** The quality of POD books, although digitally-printed, is almost indistinguishable from offset lithographic printing.

- **Who you can use.** The two main POD providers are Lightning Source and CreateSpace. The former is run by the biggest distribution company in the world, while the latter is run by the biggest online store in the world. Not bad at all!

- **Lightning Source and CreateSpace.** Both Lightning Source and CreateSpace offer a wide range of trim sizes, paper types, binding and finishes. Both also offer a dashboard facility where you can publish new titles and make changes. Lightning Source does have a wider reach in regards to distribution, but CreateSpace offers more services to authors, such as cover design and editing. They're reputable, but please bear in mind: Accept nothing short of top-notch when it comes to any service.

- **Larger investment, but higher quality and more choice.** Printing in bulk does mean a large initial investment, often in the thousands of pounds or dollars. While it may not fit directly within the realm of the Shelf Help method, bulk printing can mean lower unit costs (and therefore the possibility of a better discount for your distributors and retailers); better and more consistent quality thanks to larger print runs and offset lithographic printing; and a wider range of choices when it comes to trim sizes, paper types, bindings and finishes.

- **Bulk printing can be agile too.** To avoid the downfalls of dealing with the packaging, delivery and storage you can be clever with bulk and arrange agreements with distributors such as Gardners or retailers like Amazon. This means that instead of storing your own books and selling them by hand, you can have your printer deliver books straight to a warehouse.

- **Think outside the box.** You can also be clever and print shorter runs of your book – still getting the benefits of bulk, but reducing your initial investment. Short runs can be used for events, signings, or special editions of your book.

- And lastly, here's a list of a few **trustworthy and reputable bulk printers** that you can use, for both short runs or long runs of your book:

  - Lightning Source
  - CreateSpace
  - Blurb (for high-quality books involving lots of images, such as cookbooks, photography books, and brochures)
  - Imprint Digital
  - Troubador

Digital Publishing

Compared to print publishing, publishing eBooks is a relatively easy process. In truth, all it really involves is to upload a file and some data into the back-end of an eBook store or eBook distributor. There are no real unit costs or shipping fees to consider. There are no print-ready interior and exterior files to ponder. No book sizes, no paper types, no delivery times. It's all rather simple! (Coincidentally, this is why many self-published authors are happy to remain e-published, and dismiss print. However, I say by staying 100% digital what you're doing is actually missing out on a whole separate revenue stream, not to mention signings and book tours! Just bear that in mind as we witness the ease of ePublishing.)

That's just the tip of the iceberg when it comes to eBooks. Because of their brilliant digital nature, they can fly across the globe at the click of a mouse – effectively expanding your potential audience into the millions. Distance now has no meaning. You can be a global author without even getting up off your couch! Isn't that amazing? The sheer amount of opportunity in the digital realm never fails to astound me. But that's enough of me crowing about the wonder of eBooks. Let's first look at the two different types of eBook publishing.

Direct eBook publishing Vs eBook distribution

The direct eBook publishing model

Author creates eBook

eBook is uploaded directly to a publishing dashboard at a major eBook store

eBook is published to the store

Customers download the book onto their devices

The store handles the delivery and payments

$ – eBook store

The eBook distribution model

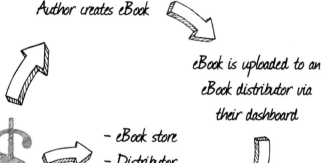

Author creates eBook

eBook is uploaded to an
eBook distributor via
their dashboard

– eBook store
– Distributor

The eBook and its
accompanying metadata is
then distributed to multiple
eBook stores

eBook is then available to
download on multiple stores.
The distributor collects all the
royalties.

The easiest way to understand the difference between these two methods is by looking at the pros and cons of both, side by side.

Direct eBook publishing

Pros

Direct control over rights, royalties, and metadata, and access to major retail stores

Changes can be made quickly, and without cost

Publishing a book is very swift – often taking under 12 hours

Royalties are paid direct, and usually monthly

Some platforms provide free conversion

Cons

Making updates to prices, rights, metadata and eBook files can be a laborious process

It can be tough to remember the ins and outs of multiple author dashboards

Separate revenue streams

eBook distribution

Pros

Authors can upload files and metadata and publish to multiple stores in just a few clicks, which means a lighter workload

One singular revenue stream, thanks to the distributor collecting your royalties for you

Usually there is no fee to use distributors – they simply take a small cut of your list price

Some distributors provide free conversion to multiple formats, such as Smashwords as well as formatting guides

Changes can be made via just one dashboard, once again meaning a lighter workload for the author

Cons

Changes to metadata and prices can sometimes cost and can also take many weeks to take affect

Publishing can often take a week or more, as the distributor has to push data out to multiple stores

Reduced control over pricing and display of metadata at the storefronts

Withdrawal from stores via distributors can often take a few weeks

Royalties are slightly reduced due to the inclusion of a "middle-man"

The great news is that you don't really have to choose one way or the other. The beauty of digital publishing is that you can easily do both! Many authors, myself included, use a combination of direct eBook publishing and eBook distribution. The reason for doing this is that it maximises coverage, enabling you to sell your book far and wide by boosting your presence. It's all down to what suits you best.

A quick note on: *exclusivity and consistency*

Some of the eBook retailers out there might offer you higher royalties in exchange for making your books exclusive to their store. An example of this is Amazon's KDP Select, an exclusivity programme that offers higher royalties in certain countries and a share of a monthly communal cash fund in return. It sounds great, but think about what you're missing out on.

*Now, I'm quite against **exclusivity** because it limits your availability and accessibility. Many authors believe that being exclusive to just one major store is enough. However, even Amazon, the biggest store, doesn't have 100% market share. By being exclusive to one store and one audience, you're effectively ignoring a great big chunk of your potential readership. This is why I promote non-exclusivity and encourage all authors to upload their books to as many eBook stores as they can manage. Of* *course, if you're going to be managing multiple books across multiple stores, you need to be...*

*...**consistent**.*

Before you do any uploading whatsoever, spend a while putting all of your book's metadata – prices, book descriptions, publication dates and ISBNs – into one handy document. Then, when uploading to different platforms, you can simply copy and paste the metadata into the relevant areas, rather than trying to remember and retype all your info. It's a lot easier and a lot more professional that way.

If the workload of managing your book across multiple stores is a worry for you, then don't worry – you can always use eBook distributors as well as going direct. (Like I said, choose the approach that suits you!) That way you only have to worry about one account and set up a title only once. But whatever you do, it's still wise to have this master document, as you never know when it will come in handy.

Direct eBook publishing

Some people say that Kindle Direct Publishing (KDP) kick-started the whole self-publishing revolution. Such a fact can never be substantiated, but I'm somewhat inclined to agree.

KDP was a bold step by an incredibly influential company and it injected the self-publishing revolution with life, energy and opportunity.

When Amazon opened its doors to self-published authors in 2007, it was doing something original. No retailer of that size had ever offered such a succinct and exciting route to market before. All of a sudden, indie authors found that they could stand side by side with traditional authors whilst taking full control of their creative destinies *and* getting an incredible 70% royalty in the bargain! KDP set a precedent for the rest of the industry and now we have several major direct publishing platforms to choose from. We're going to look at two of the best in this next section: Amazon's Kindle Direct Publishing, and Kobo's Writing Life (KWL).

KDP and KWL

Both KDP and KWL are dashboard-based. What this means is that you can log on to a private control panel with an email address and password and manage every aspect of your books yourself – from prices and the territories your book is available in to all the data that accompanies your books.

This is another brilliant aspect of ePublishing – **the ability to make changes swiftly and cheaply**. Let's say you spotted an error in your book and want to upload a corrected book file to Amazon. Not a problem! Just log on and upload the new book file and your changes will usually be made within twenty-four hours. As we saw in the **Print Publishing** section, making changes can be expensive when it comes to paperbacks and hardbacks, but with eBooks, and with KWL and KDP, there's nothing to pay. Now that's what I call agile!

Both the KDP and the KWL dashboards are very easy and quick to use and also give you access to recent sales reports. This is good, as data needs to be current as well as accurate, if we're going to put it to good use. We'll look deeper into that subject in the **Promote It** section. This means you can see how many books you're selling daily and weekly, and also where. Kobo does win by a nose when it comes to design and detail. Not that KDP's dashboard is bad by any means. Not at all. Just that Kobo offers a little more, and in a fancier way than Amazon. Have a look for yourself in any case:

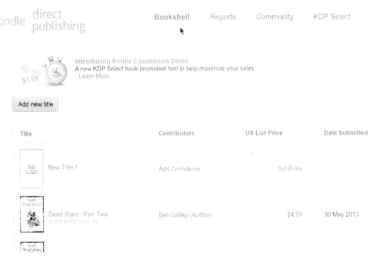

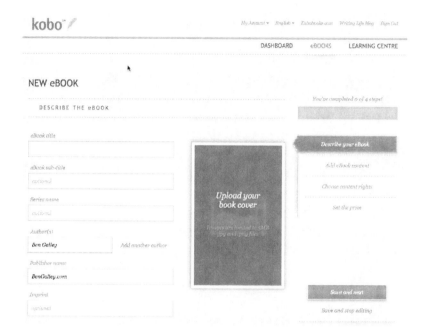

One of the most important aspects of both KDP and KWL is that these are stores with global networks and multiple websites. What does this all mean? It means they have customers all over the globe, not just in their own countries. It also means that with just a few clicks, you can sell your eBooks all over the world to all sorts of new readers. Not bad, hey? More markets, more readers, more potential for sales!

And guess what? The royalties aren't half bad either. Amazon set another industry precedent when it launched KDP. They revolutionised how much an indie author should get when a book is sold, paying out a big 70% of the list price, arguably 50-40% more than the average traditional publisher offers its authors. See, once again, more steps between you and the reader, more slices of your pie get taken. Kobo also offer 70%, and that's for all eBook prices, not just certain markets. Amazon work slightly differently. If your book is priced below $2.99 in the US or less than £1.59 in the UK, then your book will only qualify for a 35% royalty. Though, as we discussed in the section on pricing earlier, prices lower than these don't sell that well anyway, so it makes sense to stay in the 70% bracket! Amazon do also restrict royalties when it comes to selling books in certain countries, such as in their Japanese and Brazilian stores. Sales in these countries are capped at 35%. Kobo (and also others, like Google Play) don't cap according to countries.

Now when we talked about eBook formatting in the **Polish It** section, you'll remember that we discussed why it's important to get your book formatted into two different eBook formats: .mobi and .ePub. This is the moment where your dual file formats will come in handy. KDP will require your .mobi, whereas KWL will need your ePub.

The publishing process is almost exactly the same for each, and consists of the following steps:

Step 1. Create an account

Step 2. Create a new title

Step 3. Enter all the book information that is asked for

Step 4. Choose your keywords and/or categories (more on this in a moment)

Step 5. Upload your cover

Step 6. Upload your book file

Step 7. Choose your DRM option (more on this as well!)

Step 8. Set the prices for each territory

Step 9. Press publish!

And that's it. ePublishing really is that straightforward. It's easy to see why it's so popular! Just so long as you've got the formatting right and have all the information to hand before you publish, you can publish your book to a global audience in just a matter of minutes. Correction: You can become a published author in a matter of minutes. That fact never ceases to amaze me.

A quick note on: *DRM, categories and keywords*

Like most other aspects of DIY self-publishing, DRM is a personal choice. What is it? DRM means Digital Rights Management, and what it does is go some way to prevent eBook piracy and copyright infringement. DRM is technology that sits on your eBook and prevents readers who might not have legally procured a copy from viewing, copying, or sharing it. The arguments for and against DRM are vehement and ongoing. Those for DRM say it's vital in the fight against digital piracy and maintaining revenue streams. Those against say that it can inconvenience legitimate customers and also stifle innovation, and that pirates can often be your biggest fans. It's up to you to choose which side of the fence you'd like to be on. DRM or no DRM: that is your choice. Personally-speaking, I'm against DRM, but my choice might not suit you. My advice would be to read up on and investigate both sides of the argument, so that you can make the best decision for you and your books.

As we discussed in the section on metadata, categories and keywords are used at eBook stores to help readers find and discover you and your books. KWL doesn't use keywords and relies on categories instead, but KDP will ask you for both. It's really quite important to give some thought to the categories and keywords you're assigning to your book. Otherwise it might end up in an irrelevant category or be impossible to find amongst the crowded digital shelves. It's an exercise in marketing as much as it is an exercise in metadata.

Remember, it is possible to attach keywords – or tags as they can be called – to eBooks at the file level – before assigning them via a publishing dashboard. This can also help readers search for and discover your books. These can be changed, but you'll need to produce a new version of the eBook and republish, as we discussed in the **Polish It** *section.*

Of course, KDP and KWL aren't the only direct ePublishing dashboards out there. Barnes & Noble have NookPress, which was previously PubIt! – though it's only available to US authors. Google has the Google Play eBook store and offers quite a good dashboard. Apple provides a submission form for iBooks, which again is only available to US authors. And don't forget, my very own store Libiro also has a dashboard that you can use. There are also various other stores that offer submission forms or email submission, so don't be afraid to hunt around for lesser-known or specialist stores.

eBook distribution

As we saw from our earlier breakdown of the different ePublishing models, eBook distribution is a method of using one dashboard and one upload to reach multiple stores at once, even stores like Amazon, or iBooks and Barnes & Noble – stores that might otherwise be inaccessible for non-US authors. You sacrifice a little of the control and agility by adding a step between you and the reader. Nevertheless, it gives you access to stores that don't provide a dashboard and makes it easier to manage your eBooks whilst you strive for maximum coverage. Once again, there are two main providers available to us indie authors. These are Smashwords and BookBaby.

These two different from each other very slightly. Let's examine them in the usual fashion, shall we? Side by side:

Smashwords	BookBaby
Publishing is free at Smashwords	BookBaby does provide a free publishing option as well as two publishing packages – Premium and Standard
Via Smashwords you can publish your book at Amazon, Apple, Baker & Taylor, Barnes & Noble, Diesel, Flipkart, Kobo, Library Direct, Oyster, Page Foundry, Scribd and Sony	With BookBaby you can publish to Apple, Sony, Amazon, Barnes & Noble, Copia, Kobo, eSentral, Baker & Taylor, PagePusher, Scribd and Gardners Books
Free conversion to all major eBook formats via their "Meatgrinder" conversion tool, but this is dependent on meeting the formatting guidelines. These formatting guides also must be met for Premium distribution to all stores	Conversion to ePub and Mobi is included in BookBaby's Standard Package ($99) and the Premium Package ($249)
Smashwords' publishing dashboard unfortunately isn't the slickest on the market	BookBaby's publishing dashboard is more advanced and easier to use
Smashwords only take a small cut from your royalties – around 10%	Unless you pay $249 for the Premium publishing package, BookBaby takes 15% of every sale, whether you go for the free option or the Standard package
Smashwords also acts as an eBook, selling books directly to readers. For every sale at the Smashwords store, authors receive 85% of the list price	BookBaby doesn't sell books directly. It simply distributes your books to its affiliated stores.
Smashwords provides free ISBNs but these are registered to Smashwords. For $9.95, they will provide an ISBN that is registered to the author, but this is only open to US authors	BookBaby provides ISBNs at the cost of $19 – one that is registered to you. This is available to authors from any country
Smashwords doesn't provide any other services, but it does provide free formatting guides to help you format eBooks via Word (though make sure this doesn't hamper your overall quality)	BookBaby also provides promotional, cover design, and image formatting services, ranging from $149 to £279
Changes to prices, book metadata and book files are free at Smashwords	BookBaby can and do charge for changes made to eBook content. For example, 1-10 changes costs $50. Pricing and metadata are free for standard and premium (1 per year) but are $25 when using the free package

Here's my take. It's all about the ease of use. If you're going to be using a provider day-in and day-out, then you want it to be easy and simple to use. I started out on Smashwords as they distributed to two stores that can be tricky for UK authors to get access to – iBooks and Nook, but the layout and functionality of the dashboard soon took its toll on me. Though it wasn't just an aesthetic choice. When BookBaby came onto the market, I made the switch because they had more distribution outlets available, notably Gardners – which meant my eBooks got better access to the UK's non-Amazon market – and Slicebooks. They also distributed to iBooks and the Nook store, so I didn't lose anything there. Furthermore, their pricing model was better, as I could retain 100% of my royalties. Even though I knew there would be a cost with BookBaby, I believed it was worth it. Essentially I did what I thought what was best for my book.

But this self-publishing game can change quickly. Since then, however, Smashwords have added a few more outlets to their offering, such as Oyster and Scribd. And that's why I may consider using them again in the future. That's yet another beautiful thing about ePublishing, and also self-publishing in general: It's your choice. These providers are here to use, so use them whichever way you please. Or, as I may do in the near future, use both at the same time, using both distribution networks side by side, sharing the stores between them. What a wonderful digital world this is!

So in summary...

So that's eBook publishing in a neat little nutshell. You might be wondering why this section is so short, compared to print publishing, but I think it's easy to see why. Being digital in nature, ePublishing comes with all the agility and simplicity you'd expect whilst leaving the downfalls (the few that exist) of print behind. Let's recap, shall we?

- **The beauty of ePublishing comes in many forms.** The most notable benefits are as follows:

  - Negligible unit costs
  - Negligible delivery costs
  - No physical format, so no worries about storage
  - Higher royalties thanks to a lower unit cost
  - A global and instant delivery network

- **Play in the big leagues.** Thanks to the digital revolution, we now have direct access to all different kinds of eBook stores, both indie and major ones, such as Amazon and Kobo. And thanks to the invention of the publishing dashboard, we can keep direct control over every aspect of our eBooks and metadata.

- **Exclusivity or availability?** Don't forget, it's important not to be exclusive in this industry, as it means you exclude portions of your possible market, limiting your audience and potential revenue.

- **Be consistent.** Do bear in mind the need to be consistent when publishing directly to multiple stores. Keep a master document of your metadata by your side to help you.

- **Don't forget that you need an ISBN.** Assigning an eISBN is good practice and useful for search and metadata purposes. Many of the major eBook stores will ask you for one, even though they may use their own, such as in the case of Amazon and their complementary ASINs.

- **Kobo and Amazon.** The most popular direct ePublishing platforms are Amazon's Kindle Direct Publishing (KDP) platform and Kobo's Writing Life (KWL). The Amazon store will require eBooks in .mobi format, whereas Kobo, and most other stores require .ePub.

- **eBook distribution can lighten the workload.** If you're worried about the workload of managing multiple accounts and dashboards, you can always use eBook distributors instead, who push your books out to retailers much like a physical distributor. Or, if you are looking for maximum coverage and availability, you can use a combination of direct and distribution!

- **One upload. Multiple stores.** eBook distribution allows you to publish to multiple stores with just one upload. Yet making changes can be a slow affair and distribution can come with a cost – either an up-front cost or a royalty split, depending on who you use.

- **BookBaby and Smashwords.** The most popular eBook distributors in the market are BookBaby and Smashwords. Each has their own way or working, and there are pros and cons for each. Which one we choose will depend on personal preference and skill-set. However, we can use both if we wish!

Part 3 | *Promote It*

Selling that book of yours

A very warm welcome to the third and final stage of the Shelf Help method. We've come a long way already. By now, you should either be grinning ear to ear, having just published your first book, or you're on the cusp of launching into your publishing adventure. In any case, you have my warmest congratulations. You're on the path to doing something that the majority of people in this world have not, or cannot do. **The world is now your proverbial oyster.**

Whereas the first two sections of this guide have been about producing a product, this section is all about actually selling that product. Marketing and promotion are vital for making sure your book sells. Without it, your book relies on simple availability and word of mouth, which in our busy market is nine times out of ten not enough. Many authors (myself included) joke that the real work doesn't start until you actually publish your book. I'm not saying this to worry you, fear not. Instead, I'm saying this to prepare you. Marketing is not a step-by-step process like publishing and polishing can be. There is no tangible finishing line, like pressing the 'Publish' button and seeing your book appear on shelves.

Marketing involves frequent and myriad little tasks – and 24/7 effort. You have to exploit every angle you can find and keep an ear to the ground. You have to be smart and you have to persevere. This is why marketing is often referred to as an indie author's 'real job'. It's a shame really, that it takes over so much of our to-do lists, but marketing is essential for sales, and if you're clever, you can still make writing your priority. As the good Mr Edison once said:

'The three great essentials to achieving anything worthwhile are, first, hard work; second, stick-to-itiveness; third, common sense.'

So in this section, **we'll be examining your next and ongoing steps**. I'll show you a couple of ways that you can effectively market yourself and your books, using the finest technology and techniques available. Now, this isn't going to be an exhaustive nor prescriptive list. Even though I'll be explaining the methods in great detail, and also exploring alternate options in the process, the way you want to market depends on you and your book (as it should!), and there are many new methods of marketing popping up every month that goes by. Just keep both of those points in mind as we move on.

In this section I'll also give you the knowledge and skills necessary to become self-sufficient and future-proof. We'll also touch on how to balance your marketing alongside your writing, by making sure you're focusing on the right areas. And of course, in true Shelf Help fashion, we'll discuss how to stay professional too, in all your efforts.

An introduction to marketing

So what exactly *is* marketing? We know it takes effort and know-how, but what exactly do I really mean, when I say 'marketing'?

According to good old Wikipedia, marketing is this:

'Marketing is the process of communicating the value of a product or service to customers, for the purpose of selling that product or service.'

And if we dig a little deeper:

'From a societal point of view, marketing is the link between a society's material requirements and its economic patterns of response. Marketing satisfies these needs and wants through exchange processes and building long-term relationships. Marketing can be looked at as an organisational function and a set of processes for creating, delivering and communicating value to customers, and managing customer relationships in ways that also benefit the organisation and its shareholders. Marketing is the science of choosing target markets through market analysis and market segmentation, as well as understanding consumer buying behaviour and providing superior customer value.'

Distil that down and apply it to the book world and we can see that marketing has four primary goals:

1. To generate awareness and increase general visibility of you and your book,

2. To convert that awareness into sales by convincing your potential customers that your book should be purchased,
3. To forge relationships with customers, both to increase sales and build long-term, responsive communities around you and your books,
4. And lastly, to provide data about consumer behaviour, so that you can market in a data-driven, effective, way.

Of course, these four goals are united under one chief goal:

Make a living, and hopefully a good one at that.

Marketing is a beast of many faces. These days there are almost countless ways to market your books, especially now that our good friend the internet has barged its way into our lives. Marketing can be free and it can be expensive. It can take lot of effort and be really simple. It can be done on purpose, or done by accident. It can mean talking to somebody face to face, or blasting out a tweet to an audience of thousands.

The Shelf Help theory on marketing is that all these methods can be **organic** and/or **active**. Let's elaborate.

Organic and active marketing

Let's pretend we're readers for a moment, instead of authors. (This should be quite easy!) Think of your favourite book. I'll wager good money that you talk about that book whenever you get the chance. It might be once a week, or might be just every now and again, but the point is you're talking about it. Passionately too, I'll bet. A 'must-read', you might opine. 'You have to get it!', you may urge.

Who's benefiting from this? You? Not really. The person you're recommending the book to? Well, that depends on how good the book is. Instead, it's the author of the book that benefits, and possibly their publisher too. Are you getting paid for recommending this book? No, you're not. Furthermore, to the author, this is free word-of-mouth marketing. That's **organic marketing**.

Here's another example. Let's go back to being an author for a moment. Imagine that you're doing a signing in a bookshop. You're sat at a table behind a pile of your own books. It's a busy day and the shop is bustling. You catch the eye of an interested customer. (Perhaps it's Gillian!) After a courteous smile from you, they wander over and begin to peruse your table, across which you've spread your flyers and your business cards. After a bit of conversation, during which you expertly and charmingly describe your book, its contents, and the reasons the customer will love it, they hand it over for a signature and head to the till. Your efforts have resulted in a sale. This is **active marketing**.

Let's look at a few types of active and organic marketing side by side:

Active Marketing	Organic Marketing
Publishing your book to multiple stores	Readers leaving positive reviews at the storefronts
Paid advertising	A reader sharing your book with his or her book club
Sourcing reviews from blogs and online magazines	A fan leaving a comment on Facebook or Twitter
Tweeting about your book and asking for retweets	Fans liking or sharing elements of your website

You may now be wondering which type of marketing you should be focussing on. I'm pleased to say that the answer is **both**. Active and organic marketing are very much intertwined, overlapping half the time, and when used together they form a dual-pronged weapon of promotion. For instance, if that customer you met in the bookshop likes what you've written, then they may tell a friend or two. This is active marketing giving rise to organic marketing. They all feed into one another in some respect, so by tapping into as many avenues as possible and linking them all together, you will build yourself a very strong platform, one with the potential to sell a decent amount of books.

The truth is that some methods may work for you and others may not. Rest assured that a lot of marketing is trial and error and 'A/B testing'. Blogging, for instance, might be your cup of tea and snag you a load of fans in the process. But YouTube could be quite the opposite and fill you with dread. Once again, what you do is all down to your existing skill-set and the skills you can master quickly. Even though you should be trying a little of everything, don't overstretch yourself or sacrifice quality.

Now, bear in mind that some of the marketing methods above are more effective, or more powerful, than others. But there's more: **A method's power and effectiveness is also dependent on your execution**. Here's an example: Video blogging, or vlogging, is great for connecting with fans, but can be stifled by poor video quality or uninteresting content. Before you dismiss a method, make sure you've tried your best. At the same time, make sure you're putting lots of effort into the methods that do work for you. If they're working, then more power to them!

Hopefully by now, you're starting to understand what I mean by 'real work'. But let me put you at ease once more: There may be lot to do and you may not have the faintest clue about any of it right now, but by the end of this section you'll have succinct and detailed knowledge of:

- A variety of marketing methods and what each entails
- How to execute each method professionally
- How different active and organic methods work together

So without any further ado, let's move onto the next step and look at the second stage of the Shelf Help marketing theory. I call it **the funnel**.

The funnel

The funnel will not only help you understand how organic and active marketing should be applied, but also how each method fits into the overarching marketing goals we discussed a moment ago. It's also a rather handy game plan, giving you tips on how to structure and plan your marketing. You'll notice that it's not about making sales directly, but about making **friends**.

Witness the funnel.

NOISE

Interest

Subscription

Sharing

Promotion

ZEALOTS

That's funnel marketing. It's a conveyor belt where the responsibility of each cog – each marketing method – is to do two things in two stages: 1) bring fans closer to you, and therefore 2) increase their investment in you and your books, turning them into marketing machines in their own right. And this, my fellow authors, is the vital key to funnel marketing:

You're not the only one who can market your books.

This is why I always say you should be **building a 'friend base' instead of a 'fan base'**. Moving fans from the noise to the rank of friend and zealot helps you to create loyal customers, repeat customers who will actively recommend and share your book as much as you do. This is the most valuable form of marketing there is, and it's what the whole funnel is designed to maximise. It's called **word-of-mouth marketing**.

Word-of-mouth marketing is very important indeed. Think of how receptive you are to a close friend's recommendation compared to how receptive you are to an advert or a random tweet. If somebody you know – a friend, family member or colleague – recommends a certain product to you, are you more likely to listen to them, to go out and buy it? I would bet good money that yes, you are. What if the company that *made* the product recommended it to you?

Well, it's obviously biased, so its recommendation doesn't mean as much.

You see, we have become savvy to adverts and marketing messages, and this is why word-of-mouth marketing is the most powerful form of marketing today. It's why word-of-mouth marketing is found at the bottom of the funnel. It is what you should be driving every single one of your fans to do – spreading the news about your book. It's powerful. It's effective. It's what you should be aiming for.

Now let's look at one marketing method in particular and see how the shift from noise to zealot works. Let's use Twitter as an example:

NOISE

You tweet a link to your book, sharing it with the digital ether

Interest

Your link is retweeted by a fan and piques the interest of one of their followers

Subscription

The follower buys your book/explores your website and begins to follow you on Twitter

Sharing

Liking what you're doing, this new fan may then write a review or share your content

Promotion

As the relationship deepens from fan to friend they begin to actively promote you with tweets, comments, and reviews

ZEALOTS

This fan is now a zealot – a die-hard fan that will go out of his or her way to talk about you and your books, stay in regular contact, wear your merchandise and read everything you ever write.

As you can see, this version of the funnel is a rough game plan for how your marketing can be structured: **Using active marketing to drive organic marketing.**

Before we move on to discussing each method, I want to talk about an aspect of marketing that sometimes goes ignored, which is a great shame, as it's vital to the fourth goal of marketing:

'4. And lastly, provide data about consumer behaviour, so that you can market in a data-driven, effective, way.'

Knowledge is power

Modern marketing is a beast fuelled by knowledge. Data is its lifeblood. Now that we live in such a digital world, we can mine all sorts of data, and put it to very good use.

For instance, let's say you send out a tweet about your books. You may be tweeting to a thousand followers, or you may be tweeting to ten. Either way you'll want to know how effective your tweet is. You'll want to know how many people have viewed your tweet, how many clicked the link and, crucially, how many went on to buy your book. Well, luckily for us, Twitter (and a wide variety of third-party tools) can tell us those sorts of numbers.

This sort of data is marketing gold. There's a reason why corporations spend thousands, even millions, on analytics and marketing data. It's because data gives you, the marketeer, the ability to understand what is working, what isn't working, and most importantly, the reasons why. It enables you to evolve in order to market in a smarter, more effective way. By harvesting data and therefore gaining a deeper understanding, you can do a whole plethora of things! Here are a few examples of ways you can use data:

Let's say you write a blog post as part of your content marketing efforts. Once it's posted, you put the link out on Twitter and your Facebook page. On Facebook, you'll see data such as likes, shares, and general engagement. Straight away, you can tell if it's popular with your fans or not. If the data tells you it *is* popular, then you should think about focusing more on content marketing, or analyse the subject you blogged about to see if that was a reason for the post's popularity.

Let's then say that this blog is hosted on your website. If you use a good web design or hosting provider, you'll get some analytics along with your site. Monitoring your site hits before and after you post, tweet and share your blog enables you to see what sort of uplift came from it. You might even be able to see the main traffic sources. Was it Twitter or Facebook? Perhaps it was a retweet from one of your fans. Data is now telling you which is your most responsive platform.

What about your sales? Well, thanks to the data that eBook publishing providers like Amazon and Kobo provide, you can monitor your book sales before and after your blog article was posted. That way you can see whether your blogging has directly influenced sales. If there was an uplift in sales in the days following your blog post and there was little other marketing done in that time period, then the data indicates your blog may have been responsible. What can we glean? That you, fellow author, should think about posting more blog content!

Lastly, you can use data to directly influence further sales. Imagine a reader gets in touch with you and thanks you for writing such an astoundingly good book. In your reply, you can prompt them to sign up to your mailing list, to get all the news about the next book, which they're already eager to read. When the book is released, you can use their email address to tell them about it, which will hopefully lead directly to a sale. That data is powerful stuff!

So, in a nutshell:

- Data enables you to understand which kinds of marketing are working for you and which aren't. This enables you to focus on the most important methods and helps you avoid wasting time and money.
- Data allows you to be more relevant: By measuring responses, you can see what 'turns your customers on', enabling you to put out more engaging and relevant content.
- Website analytics and email addresses are some of the best types of data, so constantly driving traffic to your website and offering the option to sign up to a mailing list is very important indeed.
- Data tells you where your customers are coming from. This doesn't just mean you can tell which platform they came from, but thanks to most website analytics, you can see their country of origin, which city they come from, even which operating system they're using. You can then tailor your marketing to suit.

- Data helps you to increase your conversion rates and therefore, your sales. By analysing which methods have resulted in most sales, you can focus your efforts on them, converting your tweets, posts and blog content into more sales.
- You can also use contact information data to influence further sales. Collecting email addresses and building a mailing list is a great way to do this.

This discussion over using data brings us neatly to my **Five Golden Rules of marketing**. These rules, like the active and organic methods we'll be discussing in a moment, work in tandem with the funnel theory and govern every effort. They will help keep you focused and also help you remember to market smartly. Here we go!

The Five Golden Rules of marketing:

Now, repeat after me: **I (state your name) do solemnly swear...**

1. Always to gather data whenever possible, whatever I do and however I market.
2. Never to change two things at the same time, as it can muddy my data and analysis.
3. Always to keep my goal in mind, whatsoever it may be, so I can measure whether I've reached it or not.
4. Never to spend a single penny on marketing methods unless I'm confident that I can make it back, either in terms of sales or general awareness.

And lastly, to try everything at least once!

Now don't you forget it!

Let's move on to discussing the various active and organic marketing methods we mentioned above. First up to the plate is your website.

Be Googleable

Having a website is extremely important for us authors. Before the internet connected us all, readers had to rely on signings, tours and events to meet their favourite authors. This might not have been so bad if you lived in the same country as your favourite author. But for those readers living further afield, separated by long plane or train or car journeys, they were disconnected by distance, and therefore their level of interaction with the author was minimal – barely extending outside the pages of his or her books.

But distance doesn't matter to the internet. It smugly ignores it. Thanks to websites and social media, **we authors can connect with our readers in the blink of an eye** – even the ones who live on the opposite side of the world. We can do this on a daily basis, without even having to leave our desks. God bless the internet.

This is why you need a website. A strong (and that's a key word here) online presence allows you to be available on a global scale, twenty-four hours a day, seven days a week, fifty-two weeks a year. This availability maximises your chances of making new fans and deepens the relationship between you and your existing readers. And as theory of the funnel dictates, that's exactly what we want to be doing.

It's important to remember that a website isn't just a thing with your name on it. What sets websites apart from social media platforms such as Twitter, YouTube and Facebook is that they're controlled by *you*: you, and you alone. As you're not bound by a specific framework or a character limit, you get to dictate what goes on your website, what it looks like and what it can do. **Your website is your hub** – the place where your organic and active methods should all lead, where your reader comes to find out more about you and your books. Relevant and engaging content is therefore a must, as is keeping your website up to date and looking fresh. If you get the design and content right, your readers will keep coming back for more and each and every visit will deepen that ongoing relationship.

You'll notice that I've mentioned a few different marketing methods in this section, and this brings me on to my last point about websites. A website enables you to execute a variety of marketing techniques, all at the same time, and from just one platform. Your website can inhabit the whole spectrum of marketing at once: content marketing, social media, leveraging reviews, clever bundling and pricing. Your website can do it all, even when you're asleep! That's why it's not to be sniffed at.

Here are some tips for building your website and making the most out of it:

- **Don't fear web design.** Many believe that you need to know code if you're going to make a website, or that to do it right costs a small fortune. Again, the internet comes to the rescue. It's never been easier or cheaper to make a website. There are a whole bunch of providers out there that have simple drag and drop systems and great templates, demystifying the whole process for you. They'll also provide domain names, hosting solutions and even one or more email addresses for you. They also provide analytics and data – the whole package taken care of. You'll find a handy list at the end of this section.

- **Spend time getting it perfect.** Treat the content of your website like the content of your book. There shouldn't be a grammatical error or spelling mistake in sight and the design should be as welcoming and as professional as possible. Make sure you catch a visitor's eye with good design and a simple, modern layout. Do your research and put those templates to good work.

- **Keep it simple.** Because a website isn't constrained like other platforms are, you can do what you like with its content. However, just remember to keep it simple. A good website should be 100% killer, 0% filler. Keep the number of pages to the bare essential. You'll need a books page, an 'About you' page, a news feed or blog, and perhaps a welcome page that displays a little bit of everything to draw readers in. You can also include a picture gallery to put a face to a name. Now would be a good time to organise those professional author photos!

Whatever your website does, just remember that it needs to be the centre of your digital persona, the place where fans and friends come to find out all they can about you. It's wise to give them what they want!

- **Make it easy to share your content.** As your readers hopefully move down the funnel, towards becoming a zealot, bear in mind they will be sharing your books more and more as time goes on. You want to make it nice and easy for them. Putting 'Tweet', 'Share', and 'Like' buttons on each page and blog entry is a must.

And here are some useful website providers that you can use to create a great website. All of these providers are template-based, which means there's effectively zero code to be entered. You simply select a template you like and customise it how you want, inputting your own content. They can also provide (or point you in the right direction of) hosting for your website, domain name registration, emails and analytics. In summary, they've made web design simple for you. It's a great time to be an author, isn't it?

- Wix
- 1&1 MyWebsite
- Tumblr
- Wordpress

A quick note on: *domain names, hosting and emails*

To have a presence on the internet, you'll need a domain name. This is your little patch of the digital world and as such is identified by an 'address' or Uniform Resource Locator: that's URL to you and I.

Most of the providers above will be able to provide you with a domain name, either providing it themselves, or through a third party. This will be your website's address, so you want to keep it short and easy to remember – not something along the lines of:

www.mr-john-smith-author-extraordinaire-home-page.info.com/epic.

One way of explaining hosting is to think of it as the size of your patch. It refers to the storage of the files of your website. Each provider will likely offer you a variety of hosting options or packages, so all you have to do is pick which one suits you and your needs best. Make sure you shop around so that you know what the price band should be.

If these companies provide you with email addresses as part of their hosting or design package, then this means they'll likely be in this format:

example@authorwebsite.com

What does this scream at me? Professionalism. This example unfortunately does not:

MrOrMrsAuthor@hotmail.com

Make use of these kinds of services to nip ahead of the rest! A dedicated inbox also helps you to keep business and personal emails separate. If you're confused about how to set up emails then these providers will be more than happy to help.

The importance of being social

Twitter, Facebook, Google+, YouTube, Pinterest, Goodreads, StumbleUpon, Tumblr, Instagram, Shelfari, LinkedIn... the list goes on! There is now a horde of platforms available to us authors and all are free to use and theoretically give you access to millions of readers. The tricky part is turning that theory into a reality.

Here's a tip: **Not every platform will work for you.** This is to say that your skill-set and abilities might be better suited to one platform over another. For instance, tweeting might be right up your street, but posting photos on Instagram could be a complete mystery to you. Don't be disheartened if something doesn't feel right. Play to your strengths. There is a caveat to this point, however. Remember the fifth golden rule of marketing?

'5. Try everything once.'

With that in mind, if a platform doesn't look useful, or looks difficult, make sure you consider every angle, every application of it. Let's use the example of YouTube. You might hate getting in front of a camera, and therefore be reticent to make yourself a YouTube channel. However, you might be an illustrator in your spare time. So instead of getting in front of the camera, why not use your skills to make a book trailer? Dig deep; don't just run your hands over the surface.

Here's another tip: **Don't try to use every platform at once.** Remember your workload and that writing should be your priority. It's a hard job, staying current on multiple platforms. It's important not to pile the to-do list too high in order to have time to focus on other vital elements like writing. Make sure that you try everything once, but I would advise selecting three to five of the most useful ones and focusing on those. Any more than that, and there's a good chance you'll be driven around the bend.

Some of you might already have dipped your toes into the social media-verse. If that's you, then you might have already spotted a certain type of user in your newsfeed. Does this sort of tweet look familiar to you?

AuthorJ1981 @BuyMBookRT!
HOT NEW RELEASE: BUY MY BOOK NOW! A GREAT 5* ROMANCE AVAILBLE NOW ON KINDLE #kindle #kindleromance #ilovekindle GO BUY IT!

Expand

Imagine Twitter as a real-life conversation. Can you just image if that's how somebody talked about their book? Just blurting it out mid-sentence? That wouldn't go down to well at parties, now would it?

The truth of the matter is that a lot of authors out there – and I mean a lot – simply don't *get* social media. The clue to the whole thing is in the name: the word '**social**'. It's **social media**, not sales media. The example above is a rather obnoxious advert, not an element of conversation. To be frank, these sorts of tweets exasperate me. By all means talk about your books, but few people want to have their news feeds polluted by noisy and impersonal adverts. If you constantly act like this, you run the risk of being ignored or blocked.

Be *social* on social media. Join conversations. Strike up one of your own. Be relevant and engaging. Build upon that online persona. Remember to share content as well. This is a very important element of social media. Share other authors' tweets. Share news. Share others' posts as well as media of your own. Pictures, movies, songs, articles, links, blogs, you can share it all! Sharing reveals more of your personality because you're posting about what you find interesting and important. Those that agree will begin to engage with you, and in turn they will share your content, and start moving down that good old funnel. What you're doing here is leveraging the power behind the microcosm that social media has created – a culture as vast and varied as the cultures of the physical world, full of potential fans and friends. As you can see, social media is both active and organic.

Here're a few examples from my own Twitter feed. My tweets range from reports on what I'm up to...

Ben Galley @BenGalley · Jan 31
I'm really getting into the meat of the brand new book at the moment. Almost 50k words in, the plot's about to be turned on its head...!

Expand

...to news about the book industry...

Ben Galley @BenGalley
With Sony bowing out of the eBook game and giving their books to Kobo, should Nook follow suit? What do you think? the-digital-reader.com/2014/02/07/son...

Expand

...and from self-publishing advice...

Ben Galley @BenGalley · Dec 30
New on Shelf Help today - How to use Content Marketing in the book world. Why it's important, and what you can do! shelfhelp.info/#!How-to-do-a-...

Expand

...to stuff about fantasy and other fantasy authors...

Retweeted by Ben Galley

Joe Abercrombie @LordGrimdark
Thus she learns the taste of defeat. Thus she learns the hunger for victory. Thus and only thus shall she one day seize my spiked throne.

Expand   Retweeted

To the odd and the quirky!

Ben Galley @BenGalley · Feb 4
So... I found a fox... pic.twitter.com/EbN40rpyU

Expand   Reply   Delete   Favorite   More

Conversations will then hopefully bubble up around this content and that gives me a chance to chat to both existing fans and new people. It's great when you really think about it. I can chat to people halfway around the globe, maybe sell a book or two, and I didn't even put on my shoes.

Don't forget that social media can also be an incredibly useful feedback mechanism: my readers can read my books and then go on Twitter and personally tell me what they thought of them. (That may sound dangerous, I know, but if you've written a good book and were taking notes in the **Polish It** and **Publish It** sections of this guide, I think you'll be just fine!) It's then just a matter of forging friendships and moving them down that funnel, so they'll start sharing your content in return.

You might have noticed the spelling mistake in the example above: 'AVAILBLE' should have been spelt 'AVAILABLE'. If you publicly proclaim yourself an author, then you'll need to be on the ball with your spelling and grammar on social media. Anything less won't inspire confidence in your writing abilities. I have one rule when it comes to tweets and posts: **NO TXT SPEAK**. Zero. Zilch. Nada. Trust me on this one.

Profanity is up to you and – if used – use it wisely. Be careful about starting arguments. Do bear in mind that like you, your online persona has a reputation too. Don't be saying anything that could harm your sales. You only get one shot, so they say.

My top five platforms?

A very good question! In order, my big top five are:

1. **Twitter.** It's all about bite-sized updates and quick-fire conversations.
2. **Facebook.** This platform has more users than any and narrowly misses out on the top spot.
3. **Goodreads.** A site packed full of readers and writers, it is based around reviews.
4. **YouTube.** A great place for vlogging, or video-blogging, and for sharing too.
5. **WattPad.** Simply the biggest writing community on earth.

How to get started on social media

It really couldn't be easier. Once you've got your head around the concept of a platform, all you have to do is sign up via its website.

Now here's a tip: Make sure that when you're signing up for platforms like this, use an email address that's separate from your personal social media.

Hopefully, thanks to your web provider, you should already have a dedicated author email address, veritably gleaming with professionalism! Here's a chance to use it.

When you're choosing your username, be sure to keep it relevant to you. The golden option here in my opinion is your author name, with zero compromises, and by this I mean no letters or characters that may confuse. Making yourself easy to find can really help your fans.

Once you've signed up, the next step is to set up your profiles. And as with your book metadata, it's important to be consistent across multiple platforms. Compile a master document of all your details, such as usernames, links, your bio and your author picture, or 'promo pic' as it's often called. It's wise to make sure that this information is consistent with the info on your website too and that a good amount of thought and editing has gone into your bio.

Remember that on Facebook, it's wise to set up a Facebook Page, a dedicated profile page for businesses, artists, or anything else that takes your fancy. This helps keep your personal Facebook profile and your author page separate, which can be very handy indeed! Pages also give you analytics and the chance to take out paid advertising, which we'll discuss shortly.

Getting reviewed

At a time when the market is bursting with books, readers are increasingly dependent on reviews and lists to help them find that crucial next book. That book could be yours if you play your cards right.

Reviews are important things – they are essential to your book's success, but also very dependent on the book itself, and its quality.

Reviews are a form of **word-of-mouth marketing**, which as we discussed earlier, is a very powerful form of marketing indeed. There's a reason that sites like TripAdvisor.com are very popular: consumers want to know what other consumers think, not what a company or product is telling them. The twenty-first-century public are very aware of marketing and how it works. We're now a discerning bunch, savvy to most of the tricks of the trade. We take every slogan and tagline with a pinch of salt and because of that we sometimes bypass them and go straight to the customer reviews instead.

Reviews are doubly important. Firstly, **they help you convince customers to buy your book**. And secondly, at stores like Amazon and Kobo, **reviews also affect bestseller ranks and search results**.

So how do we go about getting reviews? This question brings us to a very important point, if not the most important point in this section:

In almost all cases, the willingness to review is entirely dependent on the book itself – its cover, its editing, but most importantly, its story.

That's right – you're actually laying the foundations for this marketing method when you're writing your masterpiece, whether you realise it or not. Here's how reviews work in practice: If a person enjoys your book, then you've done your job right and they will become a fan. He or she will then leave a review of their own accord, or alternatively they will oblige when the author asks them. This is why we worked so hard during the **Polish It** and **Publish It** sections, and why you worked so hard actually writing the damn thing. If we've written a great book, then there's a good chance of getting great reviews. But sadly, if we write a terrible book, it will likely sink to the bottom of the pile. That's another point worth remembering – **that reviews can work both ways**.

There are both active and organic ways of sourcing reviews. Organic methods range from making it easy for your fans to share, to just letting your book wow the crowd, so that they're compelled to leave a review. Active methods involve asking existing fans to leave stars and reviews at places like Amazon, Kobo, iBooks, Libiro, and Goodreads, as well as contacting review sites and publications.

To digress momentarily, there is a certain cyclical element to sourcing reader reviews. Getting more readers may mean gaining more reviews, but to get more reviews you need more readers. Catch 22, anyone? The process just goes around and around in a circle, **so sourcing reviews is also dependent on where a fan sits in the funnel** – those further down, your friends toward the zealot end, will be more likely to leave you a review if you ask them. In the true spirit of overlapping organic and active methods, this means you can use other sorts of marketing to make sourcing reviews easier. Hopefully that should give you a few sneaky ideas!

So in a simple nutshell, sourcing reviews is a reader-by-reader process, one that is heavily influenced by your book's quality, opinion, how close a fan is to you and your own effort. Reviews can be bad and they can be good. Therefore reviews aren't a 100%-guaranteed method of selling books. But when they work, they can really work.

One review, in the right spot and at the right time, can be incredibly effective. A hundred reviews might sell just one book, but there's always that one review that can sell a hundred. That's why you've got to keep at it, aiming for that big punch, that word-of-mouth.

So how exactly do you source a review? I believe you can split reviews into four types and each can be sourced in different ways:

The four types of reviews

The starred review

At most eBook stores, titles are accompanied by stars or ratings. These are supplemental to media and POS reviews, and for a consumer they're a great snapshot of what the masses think. There are two aspects to starred reviews: How many there are, and the overall score. High numbers for each are what you're aiming for.

How do we source these? Active: Ask your fans! Organic: Simply make sure your books are featured on sites with a star-rating system, like Amazon and Goodreads.

The media review

Media reviews are those found on book or genre websites, social platforms like Goodreads or Twitter, in the printed or digital press. Depending on the size of the readership and the reach of the reviewer, site or publication, media reviews can be crucial for sales and reputation. (Bear in mind that this does work both ways!)

How do we source these? Active: Media reviews are difficult to obtain, as many blogs and publications simply say no to any self-published work, or will only review bestselling books. All you have to do is keeping searching and emailing. Organic: Nothing organic this time, except relying on that good old worth-of-mouth.

The POS review

These are reviews left at stores, directly next to, above or below your book. POS means Point Of Sale, and being included beside your book it makes it very convenient for anyone browsing the shelves. Don't forget these also contribute to rankings and searches.

How do we source these? Active: ask that friend base again via your website, your social media, or by using your mailing list. Organic: Once again, make sure your book is available at stores such as Amazon and Kobo. Make sure your book is on Goodreads too, as sometimes Goodreads reviews are fed to stores.

The cover review

These are reviews similar to POS, designed more for physical books and bookshops, though you can include them in your metadata too. Ideally, a cover review should be a review from an impressive or renowned source, such as another well-known author or reputable publication. When a customer picks up your book in a bookshop, or scans your blurb at an online store, that opinion, which will seem quite independent, will carry with it a lot of weight and be very convincing indeed.

How do we source these? Active: firstly you need a review from a good source and that can be hard to get hold of. Get emailing again and try to forge some contacts in the social media-verse. Organic: if your book does well, it might naturally attract a high-profile reviewer that actually gets in touch with you. If you get a quote you can use, you could either republish with an updated cover or add it to your metadata.

Hopefully, once the good reviews start rolling in, it's time to put them to good use. Display them on your website, put them on your book cover, share them on your Twitter and Facebook, the whole lot!

A quick note on: *sock-puppetry and paid reviews*

No, I haven't gone mad. Sock-puppetry is the term given to deplorable practices such as paying up front for positive reviews, creating fake accounts and writing your own reviews, and/or using fake accounts to leave bad reviews for your competitors' books. It's utterly unethical and has somewhat undermined some of the power behind reviews. Sock-puppetry first came to light in early 2012, when several bestselling authors were named and shamed as sock-puppeteers. The uproar was somewhat deafening, I can tell you! The reason I'm telling you this is because I want to advise you against it. Not that I imagine you're considering it, but I just want you to be wary of its existence, and understand why it's bad.

Paid reviews are slightly different, and the service is quite a common one. There are many reasonably reputable companies out there who will charge you a fee for the chance of a review. This might seem quite attractive when you start looking into how reputable these companies, or their reviewers, are, and where they can have your review posted. I've been tempted in the past, but the truth of the matter is that paying for reviews seems too much of a wasteful expense to me. As these companies are ethical compared to sock-puppeteers, they aren't able to guarantee a good review, so you could be lining yourself up for a fall if their one reviewer doesn't like your book. What I'm saying is that it's not a fair representation of your book and can end up being a costly mistake. Take that into consideration when you're having a look around the net.

Going digital

Here's a very simple and quick method for you!

One of the best ways of getting you and your book out there is **simply to get you and your book out there**. Reviews aren't the only way of getting mentioned on sites and blogs. Whatever your genre, subject or area of expertise, there are plenty of websites out there where you could do interviews, write a guest blog, host a giveaway or competition... or whatever else springs to mind! There are all sorts of things you can do. It's all up to you and the sites you get in contact with.

The internet has given us a marvellous gift – a vast expanse of websites, of all different sizes and subjects. And in the digital world, **it's all about presence**. The more websites you feature on, the higher your chance of being noticed and being clicked on. It's the same reason behind getting your books into multiple formats and stores. It's easy to see that just like reviews and attending events, a digital presence can be a great way of marketing your books. Just remember:

If it can't be seen, it can't be sold!

So how do we go about building a digital presence? Three things: Content, research and email.

First off, you need to be thinking what it is you can offer websites and blogs. Is your book interesting in some way, other than its contents? Is there a story behind how you wrote it? Can it help people? Do you yourself have an interesting story? Would an interview with you be intriguing to a certain audience? What you're doing here is finding your unique selling point, your USP. In other words, the reason why a site would feature you. Once you have your content and your USP, it's only a simple matter of going out and finding the sites and blogs you want to feature on, both large and small.

My advice here is to look for sites that relate directly to you and your books, or the subjects and genres you write about – sites that would find your content interesting.

Now's the time to think outside the box. For instance, let's say I've written a book about my incredible journey around the world in search of the hottest hot sauce known to humanity. I wouldn't just look at the sites about literature, I'd be talking to travel websites and cooking blogs as well.

Once you've gathered up all the contact details for the sites you've chosen, it's time to get emailing. Remember to be clear and concise in your introduction, telling your story and explaining why you're emailing them in just a few short paragraphs. Be open to any opportunity and include links to more information. Cast your net and then reel them in.

Another thing you can do is a blog tour. Just as travelling from one bookshop to the next in the real world helps to build your fan base, so does touring blogs. All you need to do is set up a series of appearances – reviews, interviews, competitions, guest blogs, whatever you can – which occur in close succession, just like a tour. If you're clever, you can hit networks of blogs – blogs that are united by a genre or a specific subject. For instance, many fantasy review sites work together in close-knit communities. A blog tour of these can really help you cover all bases and maximise your potential presence!

Content aplenty

Content marketing is the term used to describe a broad range of different marketing methods. Content marketing is therefore a bit of a shape-shifter. It can take the form of blogging, vlogging, videos, trailers, guest blogs, interviews, news feeds, infographics and free samples or downloads.

Put very simply indeed, content marketing is the creation and publication of content, either text or media-based. **The Content Marketing Institute** puts it best:

'The aim of content marketing is to inspire loyalty in your consumers and readers, by delivering "consistent, ongoing, valuable information".'

In my opinion, the objective of content marketing is to stimulate a response in your fan or curious internet user.

This could be any number of responses, such as anger, laughter, awe, surprise, or simply increased interest in you, the author. What's the point of creating such responses, I hear you ask? Well, the more stimulating your content, the higher the chance that this person will **share** your content. This is word-of-mouth, as plain as could be. That's why whatever content you produce, you need to:

Make it share-able

And also…

Point it straight back to your website

That's the secret to content marketing, in my eyes. By creating something that people can't help but share and making your web address suitably prominent, you're spreading your name across the social media-verse. The result? Let's do a little maths:

More shares = Higher chance of visits.
More visits = Higher chance of sales.

First, capture some hearts and minds and then lead them swiftly down that good ol' funnel.

Content marketing may seem like a strange, indirect beast, I'll be the first to admit it. After all, spending time actively producing content that isn't your next book might seem a little counter-productive. That's why I always recommend balancing your time wisely, as with all marketing activities. But this content can surround you and your books with a halo of engaging media, all of which serves to capture the attention of new readers and bring them straight to where you want them: on your website, taking a good hard look at you and your books. That's the real trick behind content marketing.

So how exactly do we get content marketing right? Well first you need to think outside your books: Can you make video-based content, or are you better at blogs? Could you organise a clever freebie? Provide a few handy tools or guides? It's time to get creative and to make use of the skills you have and could learn quickly. It's all about being clever and quirky too, about being bold, but not leaving too much of a gap between your extra content and your core offering.

Here's a handy little example for you: We're going to pretend we're an online store that sells all sorts of fitness-related products – protein powders, vitamins, supplements, clothing and the like. We want to add a little more value to our site and so we're going to do something clever and bolt an advice section onto our store. We're going to pack it full of helpful articles and videos featuring personal trainers and nutrition experts. We're even going to include a few little tools too, like workout builders and even a handy BMI calculator. Why? Because **it will increase trust and loyalty in our customers**. Furthermore, it will make us helpful and useful, and encourage people to stay on our site for longer, giving us more of a chance to show them our attractive products.

Here's a specific example for us authors: Let's imagine you're an author of a humorous and scandalous tale of your time in the fashion industry. You want to do a little content marketing. How about blogging about current scandals in the fashion industry, or tweeting about fashion news? You could even release a little photo-book of the best fashion moments of history! Here's an idea: Why not offer it as a free download on your site and make sure it points to your main novel? You're doing something nice for your existing and potential fans, so **they'll be much more inclined to buy and appreciate your book.** More shares, more sales, more reviews!

You can do some clever things with content marketing. It's all about being smart and creative. It's about being different and yet still keeping whatever you produce relevant to you and your book. Remember: **Make it share-able.** That's the funnel in action – content marketing is a very *active* method, but it can lead to some really great *organic* opportunities if your content is compelling enough.

Just remember that whatever content you produce, it must be shared far and wide. Tweet about it, post about it, write, talk and email people about it.

It doesn't matter how astounding your content is – if nobody ever sees it, it's useless.

Using emails

As we discussed in the section about data, collecting email addresses is a very useful thing to do. The reason for collecting emails, or in other words – **building a mailing list** – is that it helps you keep your subscribers up to date. As I mentioned earlier, you can use mailing lists to let your fans know about a new book, but you can also use mailing lists for general updates and to keep them moving down the funnel. Tweets and posts are great, but they can get lost in the noise of the social media-verse. Emails are delivered by hand, so to speak, directly into the inboxes of your friends and fans. You can even personalise emails, making their content more relevant. And don't forget, **the reason you have a fan's email address is that they gave it to you**. This means they're interested in you, so you have a good chance of getting a higher response rate.

This is why building a mailing list is very important – it's a method of marketing that can pack a powerful punch when combined with other methods, such as content marketing or specific campaigns.

In truth, using a mailing list is a form of content marketing, insofar as you'll need to produce content to mail to people. The reason I'm talking about it as an individual method is that this content can be separate from whatever secret projects you've got simmering away underneath the content-marketing umbrella.

Mailing lists can be used for newsletters and important updates, sharing blog posts or video posts, your latest clever content-marketing idea, or for promoting new books, special offers and competitions. You could even promote a little more word-of-mouth marketing while you're at it and ask for some reviews. It's up to you. The only things you need to worry about are collecting those precious little email addresses and the content you're putting into your emails. Just be sure to stay relevant and interesting. And don't forget: There are laws governing spam and mailing lists; **if somebody wants to unsubscribe, then you honour that request!**

Collecting email addresses can be done by including a mailing list sign-up form on your website or blog, or by taking a sign-up sheet to events and signings. If you're looking for a few good ways to manage your mailing list and send professional-looking emails, have a look at providers like **MailChimp** and **RapidMail**.

Let's get physical

Just as print books shouldn't be ignored, neither should physical marketing. I'm not talking billboards and adverts on the side of buses here, or TV and radio adverts. These methods are almost always out of reach for us indies. They cost far, far too much. No, what I'm talking about are physical methods of marketing that can support and feed into your digital marketing. While bookshops and print books still exist I believe it is worth getting physical. The sorts of physical marketing I'm talking about are:

- Local and (possibly) national press
- Merchandise available at signings and from your site
- Posters or flyers in bookshops and at signings

Don't be worried by the apparently wide scope of physical marketing – we'll be examining each one in turn soon.

A quick note on: *digital data in a physical world*

In the meantime, some of you might be wondering about how you're going to **harvest precious data** in this physical world. This is good – you're in the marketing frame of mind! The good news is that there are still many ways you can be physical and yet remain digital too.

Whatever the primary goal of your physical marketing – be it advertising an event, a new book, or simply talking about yourself – I believe you should always focus on doing two things (aside from selling books, that is). We discussed both of these earlier. **The first is driving traffic to your website**, where you can let your eye-sizzlingly good design and slick wording work their magic. **The second is to collect email addresses**, that all-important form of data, so that you can build up your mailing list and deliver vibrant and engaging content directly to those who have deemed you interesting. Here are a few tips on how to do these two things:

- Make a mailing list sign-up sheet and take it to your events and signings, so that customers can sign up for more information or news.
- A QR code is basically a type of barcode which can be read via the cameras on mobile devices and link directly to a URL. Including these on your posters will enable customers to access your content on the go,

rather than having to remember it later. You can even put them in your books to create web traffic out of bookshop traffic.

⦿ *Lastly, mentioning or including your web address or Twitter username at every available opportunity can help people find you and help them take a step down that funnel. Though QR codes are simple and direct, some people might not know what they're for, so you need a backup: your www web address!*

Let's look at these physical marketing methods in turn.

Local and national press

This kind of marketing sits at the very top of our funnel and can be quite effective, depending on the readership, genre, and punch of the publication.

It goes without saying that the bigger the newspaper or magazine, the harder it is to be featured in. Physical press is somewhat more difficult to crack than digital press and blogs. This is primarily down to two facts: that space on a printed page is a valuable thing these days, and that it is reserved for the stories that journalists deem relevant and interesting. What this means is that papers and magazines, especially the larger ones, might not be willing to include a story about an unknown book by an unknown author. Of course, if you are of some renown, perhaps a successful traditional author turned indie, you might have better luck. In any case, you'll need a hook, a story. Think of it like this:

Why should journalists be telling their readers about you?

My original angle, which has sadly crumbled a little in recent years, is my age. At twenty-three, I had just released my first book and it was already selling in a major Waterstones bookshop (I'll tell you more about that in a moment). When I told the local paper, *The Surrey Times*, they were quite intrigued and agreed to put out the story in their weekly newspaper. Fortunately for me it was a story they thought quite interesting, and, thanks to that article, I went on to get quite a lot of press coverage, especially as I could offer some self-publishing tips too. Thanks to that first step, I've done interviews for *BBC Sussex* and *BBC Radio 2* and featured in articles in *The Guardian*, *Forbes*, and *The Sunday Times Magazine*.

The trick is to find your own angle. Perhaps your book is a powerful personal tale. Perhaps it's a riotously funny satire of current events. Perhaps it's the first, or the last, or the best, or the biggest. **Find your USP** – your Unique Selling Point, and use that in your pitch to journalists. It's then just a matter of time, emails and effort.

Merchandise

'Merchandise' can mean many things to many people. Many authors unfortunately forget all about it – dismissing it as something you get at gigs or concerts, or if you're a big *Star Wars* fan. I say different. Merchandise should have a place in an author's marketing toolbox and I'm going to tell you why.

I believe that there are two types of merchandise: **takeaway merchandise** and **premium merchandise**.

- **Takeaway merchandise.** Badges, business cards, pens, key rings, bookmarks, and stickers – these are all examples of what I like to call 'takeaway merchandise'. They are inexpensive and can be given away for free. This is what makes this kind of merch 'takeaway'. The reason this is important is because everybody likes getting something for free. A badge might only cost you 10p, but a fan will see it as a little piece of treasure, a memento. It's something they got when they met that amazing author that time.

- **Premium merchandise.** T-shirts, hats, hoodies, posters, prints, phone cases – these are examples of premium merchandise. Premium merch does have a higher cost, hence the name, and it is something that your fans and friends need to invest in. It's more for the zealot-end of the funnel, but it can create a whole new revenue stream for you. Premium merch does take a little more effort and know-how, but if done right it can work very well indeed.

Please do bear in mind that when you're designing your merchandise, you need to create something that somebody will be eager to wear and to show off. There is a big reason for this, besides simply making a sale:

Your merchandise is a walking advert for you, your brand and your books.

Think of it like this: When a fan wears one of your badges, and is hanging out down at the local coffee shop, somebody might say, 'Hey, what's that badge for?' Lo and behold, a conversation about you and your books is about to begin and I'd wager that a little bit of word-of-mouth marketing is about to get done. Maybe it will result in a book sale or two! Isn't that great? And all you did was get a few badges made! So as you can see, actively producing and sharing merchandise can result in some great organic opportunities.

Getting this merchandise to your fans can be done in a variety of ways. The two primary ways of getting merch out there are selling it direct from your site and handing it out personally at events and signings.

Posters and flyers

Posters and flyers are a really simple way of getting the word out about you, your books and any events you have coming up. The application of this marketing method is really quite simple: Always put up posters and flyers in places that give you the maximum impact or return; in other words, the most relevant places possible.

Posters and flyers straddle a few sections of the funnel. They can be noise to some, but to others, to friends and zealots, they serve to inform and keep fans engaged.

There are two things to put thought into when using printed advertising material: Firstly, your **design**; secondly, the **cost**.

Whether you design the content of your flyers and posters yourself, or you use a designer, keep your goals in mind. What is this poster trying to achieve? How will it achieve this? What information will you need to include? How can I collect that all-important data?

Just like your book cover, posters and flyers have a job to do. This job is selling. Don't forget: you can use QR codes (which can be generated by online services such as Kaywa). Whatever you do, make sure you have your URL prominent!

Unless you already have the ability to print flyers and posters to a professional standard, printing physical material will likely cost you a little bit of money. It shouldn't be too much, but it will depend on who prints them. Make sure that when you're finding a printing company, ask for samples of their print quality and for a quote up front. Remember, when spending any money, analyse what return you're likely to get. If you're 100% sure it's an acceptable cost, by all means, go ahead!

So where exactly do you put these posters and flyers? Essentially, anywhere you can! It makes sense to put your posters or flyers in places a) where they will be seen, and b) which are relevant to the intended audience and/or event. For instance, if you've got a signing coming up in a local bookshop, don't put all your posters up forty miles down the road. That just doesn't make sense! Instead, ask if you can put them up in the bookshop and any surrounding stores. Market smart!

Signings and events

Signings

Signings hold a special place in every author's heart. Much like getting your books onto a bookshop's shelf, signings seem to be a mark of validation, a step up the ladder of success. Perhaps it's the fact you're sharing floor space with the greats and the classics. Perhaps it's just the simple truth that a bookshop has actually let you in, given you a table and given you free reign. Perhaps it's the fact that you get to sign your book in public and see the satisfied face of your newest reader. Or maybe it's because you get to sit (or stand!) behind a pile of your own books all day and if you're smart, get to watch that pile dwindle to an empty space. I'm going with a mix of all four.

I thoroughly enjoy signings. I've been lucky enough to do a couple of UK tours. I've met some fantastic people along the way and a great many new readers too. The great thing about meeting your fans in person is it means they are more likely to move down that ol' funnel – and more quickly too. Once again, active marketing is leading straight to organic marketing. That's the funnel working perfectly.

How to go about organising a signing

You can either organise an event yourself, at a venue of your choosing, or you can apply to a bookshop. There are pros and cons for both. For instance, busy bookshops mean lots of traffic for your table, whereas organising an event yourself means you have to put the work in to summon an audience. Bookshops will take a cut. With events you also have to bear venue hire in mind.

It's once again down to what suits you. Many of you might be able to rustle up a hundred attendees. Others might not. My strength is having a great relationship with the staff at a number of bookshops. Find out where your strength lies and play to it!

Getting into indie bookshops and bookshop chains

Getting into indie bookshops is definitely easier than getting stocked in bookshop chains, but it will always depend on your book, your sales figures and your conduct.

Firstly, your book has to be sellable and this is where your professional book cover and editing comes in handy. It will also need that all-important ISBN and a barcode too. When dealing with a chain, your book may also need to be available from a certain distributor. This shouldn't be an issue if you've chosen to work with a good POD printer or distributor. Or else, they may just take the books directly from you, but this is much more likely at indie bookshops.

Any sales figures, if you have them, will also come in useful. Remember that by ordering your books in (which may not be sale or return), the bookshops hope to sell them on for profit. Let them know what margin they can expect. Give them those all-important numbers. Remember, as we said earlier, the higher the better!

Your conduct will matter too. A moment ago I mentioned that I had a great relationship with the staff at my local major bookshop. That's right, your funnel applies here too! By sincerely befriending bookshop staff, they will be more likely to understand your professionalism. If they're interested in what you've written, then you can always offer them a free copy. If they like it, they may be willing to stock it.

Bear in mind that many shops, especially big chains, have policies about unknown books. If you get turned down for this reason, remember that it isn't personal, it's just policy. Be gracious, and thank them for their time.

If and when your books have made it onto the shelf, you have to make sure they sell – like hotcakes. That way you prove the value of your books and you prove you're capable. It's at this point that you can politely enquire about doing a signing.

Successful signings

Here are several important things to remember when doing a signing, especially if it's your first:

- **Early advertising**. Make sure you use your posters and flyers ahead of, and during, the event. Don't forget to use your takeaway merch too.

- **Order wisely.** If you're in charge of the stock, be smart about how many of your books you order. You don't want to run out, but you don't want to be stuck with a huge pile at the end of the day either.

- **Effort for profit.** If your bookshop would like to order the stock in, bear in mind they want to make a profit. This means you need to make an effort for them as well as yourself.

- **Cash.** When organising your event, think about how you're going to handle cash. You might want to get yourself a little mobile card reader, or a secure money tin.

- **Don't forget your manners.** Be polite and professional to staff and customers. If you're signing at a bookshop, don't be rude and forceful with customers. If they don't want to buy your book, so be it. Thank them anyway! Too many indies have caused trouble at major bookshop chains by having the wrong attitude. Make sure this isn't you. Be extra nice to the staff too, as they're the ones who have been kind enough to put you up, and will be the ones recommending your books after you leave.

Politeness costs nothing, after all, and your reputation is always fragile.

- **Connections matter.** Always remember to mention your website, email address, or Twitter handle if possible. Give these new readers a reason to connect with you besides how good your book is. Don't forget your mailing list sign-up sheet!
- **And a comfortable pen!** Don't forget to Practise your signature, and don't forget to get yourself a nice, comfortable pen!

Events

Now, don't forget that signings aren't the only events on the menu. As an author it's wise to attend as many events as feasible. Book conventions, book fairs, author conferences, industry events, and workshops – there's always something going on, and there's almost always an opportunity to be discovered. Like they say in the music industry:

'It's not what you know, it's who you know.'

The same is true of the book industry. It's important to make some contacts, and these could take the form of industry professionals, other authors editors, designers, reviewers, journalists, bloggers and of course, your readers. Events are perfect places for running into such a person.

Why is this important? Well, the possibilities are endless. Who knows who you'll happen to run into at a book fair or a convention, what opportunities they might represent? I've met some really great people over the last few years, people whom it would have been impossible to meet if I hadn't put my shoes on and attended a few events. These people have opened doors and put me in places at which I would have laughed in disbelief a handful of years ago. Each and every person has helped me in some way, and I them. It's a great industry, and the only way to embed yourself in it is, well, embedding yourself in it.

You can also achieve this by featuring at events, as well as attending. By actively requesting, or by organically creating contacts, you may be able to land speaking, signing or panel opportunities at various events in your genre or field. Once again, as with building a digital presence, you'll need a story, an area of expertise, or at the very least, something to say. Ask yourself the question – **why should I get booked for this event?** If you know you've got a solid answer, then get emailing.

Taking part in events is really important for getting your name out there – and let's not forget your book titles too. Whether you're making contacts or making fans, I'd highly recommend it!

Paying your way

Now, I'd like to mention paid advertising, as it is an important thing to learn about. Although we're striving for affordable solutions here, some paid advertising methods can be cheap and can actually pay off. That's why I think it's important to cover.

Paid advertising is a very active method of marketing, but as with many of the methods in this section, it can lead straight to organic opportunities if you play your cards right.

And that's the crux of it. You can't just throw your money at something – you'll just end up wasting money. To avoid that fate, you need to put in some deep thought and planning time. And lots of it! If you want paid advertising to work for you, keep the following in mind:

- **Cost versus return.** Don't just pay for something without analysing the benefit. If you're shelling out for something, you should be very confident that you're going to make your money back, either in sales or word-of-mouth.

- **Assess what it is you want to achieve.** Make sure your ads have a definite purpose: a 'call to action'. Make that purpose clear in all ads and press releases.
- **Wording and design.** Make sure you also put a little effort into the wording and design of any ads as well. This is important.
- **Sharks.** There are companies out there that will sell you the moon and deliver only dust. Make sure you put in some long, hard thought regarding any company you work with.
- **Keywords, search terms and demographics.** Targeting is extremely important. If you're not reaching the right people, then all your work will have been for nothing. Think long and hard about keywords, search terms, and demographics, to ensure your ads are being placed in front of the right people.

There are many different kinds of paid advertising, so what I've done for you is compile a list of the main methods. It's not exhaustive by any means, but it'll give you a good idea of what we're talking about. Here we go:

Pay per click

Pay-per-click advertising (PPC, also called CPC, or cost per click) is a method of marketing by which you broadcast a range of text or image-based adverts across search engines and websites. For the pleasure, you pay an amount of money every time that somebody clicks on your advert. The more clicks, the more you pay.

Sounds dangerous, right? Well, luckily there are usually safeguards in place. Google AdWords is a prime example of PPC marketing. You can create campaigns that will either display text-based ads next to search results, or show image-based ads on websites of your choosing. Where your ads appear and how well they perform is up to you, but it means managing almost a dozen separate elements, some of which you can control and others you can't, such as human behaviour.

What you do have control over is the 'targeting' of your campaigns, which is difficult in itself. It involves writing the ads, setting keywords, making sure you're not wasting money… It can involve a large amount of work. Trust me, I've been tinkering with AdWords for many years now! It is for these simple reasons – its complexity, unpredictability and potential cost – that I usually advise steering clear of PPC advertising. However, if you've got experience in this area, or spot a niche, then by all means, dive right in! Just beware of the potential costs.

There are other PPC providers besides AdWords, such as Bing Ads. It's also not uncommon to find companies that can provide ad placements in specific niche markets or genres, such as fantasy, sci-fi, romance, or erotica. Keep an eye out for them!

Pay per impression

Pay per impression (PPI, also called CPM, or cost per thousand impressions) is very similar to PPC, but what you're paying for here is the number of times your advert appears on a website. What PPI providers do (again, they can be both niche, market-specific providers or larger companies) is take your adverts and distribute them to their PPI network of websites. Depending on how much you pay, (usually per thousand impressions, or in other words, how many times an advert is seen), your advert will be displayed in designated spaces on websites usually related to the subject of your campaign. Once again, these may be targeted by you, or set by the PPI provider.

However, the big, resounding problem with PPI is that you have no idea if anybody has interacted with your ad or not. You're never quite sure if it's being seen at all. All you've got to go on is the strength of the PPI network and the traffic on the sites your ad features on. That's pretty much it.

Now as you can imagine, I don't normally recommend PPI. Nevertheless, sometimes you will find a good company, a good deal, or even just a great niche.

I used it to advertise my Kickstarter graphic novel project at the beginning of February. I used a small company to get my ads shown on a busy network of gaming and comic book websites and blogs. It was cheap, around $50, and resulted in a good percentage of traffic, which went on to bring in just under 20% of the pledges.

Conceivably, if I hadn't used PPI, I wouldn't have hit my target of £5,000. I attribute the success of that PPI campaign to good targeting, a reputable company and good looking ads, which I had a designer make for me. Overall cost? Definitely less than the estimated £1,123 the PPI campaign brought me!

Adverts in magazines and on websites

Once again, this sort of advertising can be expensive, but depending on the readership of the publication, either digital or physical, you may have some luck!

What it all comes down to is targeting, your message, and, ultimately, the price. This is why I would recommend getting some good-looking ads together. And go for the niches too. For instance, your local paper will probably have a very general audience, which isn't good in terms of targeting. Look instead for magazines or website that directly relate to the genre or subject of your book. That way you've got a higher chance of making some fans as you'll be more relevant and eye-catching.

Another place you can buy adverts is in the hand-outs or gift bags at conventions or events. There's a veritable plethora of opportunities here, and not just the usual suspects like the fantasy (guilty), sci-fi, horror, erotica, romance, and crime conventions. There are also plenty of industry events on an author's calendar. There may be some opportunities there! Normally you can pay to have a flyer or hand-out inserted, or buy space in the convention guide. Once again, it all comes at a cost. This could be designing, printing, delivery, insertion, or simply the cost of the space on the page. All you have to do is tally up all the costs and weight them against the potential gain.

Goodreads also offers advertising solutions. Whenever your ads are clicked, your bid is deducted from a pre-paid balance. Once again, any success and costs are dependent on your targeting, what you're advertising and how you advertise it. Give it some thought!

Facebook and Twitter ads

Now here's a method I use regularly. Why? Because for what you normally get in return, the cost can be quite low. It's also a very agile system of paying for ads, jam-packed with analytics and stats.

Facebook offers two ways you can pay your way. First of all, you can boost posts. You need to accrue more than fifty likes before you can boost anything, but once you've done that you'll see a little option next to each status, photo, or link you post, reading '**Boost post**'. If you click on that you'll be presented with a range of prices with corresponding reach. What you're paying for here is for your post to appear in the news feeds of your likes and their friends. I use it if I have an important announcement or a milestone I want to shout about. Depending on how many likes you have, you can usually reach a couple of thousand people for under $20.

The other type of paid advertising you can do on Facebook is the general marketing of your page. Ever wondered about those little adverts on the right-hand side of your Facebook page? This is what you'll be paying for, and it can cost a little bit more than boosting posts. Essentially, you're paying for the opportunity for likes. You'll see an option for this on your Facebook Page dashboard: 'Promote this page'. Both options – boosting posts and promoting pages – come with a serving of in-depth analytics on the side. These can be really useful indeed for assessing whether your ads have worked.

Twitter Ads runs a little bit like AdWords, where you can promote your account or a specific tweet. Once again, you set a daily budget, target your audience, then set a maximum bid price. If your bid is high enough, your ads will appear in the timelines of your audience. Simple as that! You'll only pay if somebody interacts with the ad, or if others retweet, reply, or follow you. The handy thing about Twitter Ads is that they too provide in-depth stats on your ad performance, making it really easy for us authors to track how we're doing.

Adverts on radio, TV and public transport

I'm not going to give these methods much of a mention at all, as I'm of the opinion that they're usually ridiculously expensive. We're trying to run a business here – we want to keep our marketing affordable. Shelling out for big adverts is pretty much a no-no. Adverts like these can cost hundreds of thousands, so if you haven't got the cash, just forget about it!

Marketing agencies

There are many companies out there who can help you to market your books. This is an area of paid advertising that can be very hit and miss and it will almost always come down to which company you choose. What market agencies will normally do for you is send out press releases to their various contacts, pushing for reviews, interviews, and mentions. These contacts could be press, radio, TV, or even event organisers. A good example of this sort of company is Authoright. New Generation Publishing also offers press release and marketing services.

Some marketing agencies can even handle the social media for you, or any further paid advertising such as promotions or physical marketing. You could be paying for a whole variety of things here: The work taken off your plate, the creation of a professional press release, profiles, campaigns and hopefully that glowing plethora of contacts in the agency's little black books.

Personally-speaking, I've never used a marketing agency, as in my eyes the cost usually outweighs the gain. Marketing agencies can be expensive and I've always been reticent to invest such a lump sum. Don't forget, it is possible to make contacts of your own, and build a press release. It is a bit of a skill, but it can be learnt. I think it's time for that favourite phrase again:

It all depends on you and your books!

Pricing, giveaways and competitions

These three also fall into the marketing category as they are ways of gaining new readers, climbing charts, and increasing your overall visibility.

Pricing

Pricing can be used in a clever way. We're talking eBooks here. Thanks to the wonder of the internet and platforms like KDP and KWL, we can change our prices very quickly and very easily. We can drop prices for special events or holidays, or even raise them slightly when you're seeing a lot of interest and sales. Keeping your eye on your competitors' prices is wise too. So is keeping an eye on the average price of books in your market or genre. Pricing is very personal and there are lots of ways to use pricing to your advantage. Whatever you do, it's up to you!

Giveaways and 'perma-free'

In 2013, I released the third and fourth books in 'The Emaneska Series'. With four books on the market, all priced at around $3.99, I decided to try giving away my first book *The Written* for free, to test whether it would increase sales of the series as a whole. I wasn't planning to give it away free for long, nor was I expecting a gigantic uplift. I was hoping for one, of course, but if marketing teaches you anything, it's to be conservative with your expectations!

After I set my first book free on Kobo, Amazon soon set it free as well. In a week, roughly 10,000 copies were downloaded. The week after, the numbers kept on rising. Thanks to the success of that one giveaway, *The Written* is now a 'perma-free' book, and the uplift in sales, reviews and fans has been very noticeable indeed.

I would definitely recommend organising giveaways of your books, but I wouldn't recommend doing too many, or for too long. *The Written* will be given a price again soon, that much I know, but in the meantime, the giveaway is working. As soon as my data tells me it isn't, I'll be stopping it. (Another feather in the cap of data!)

Of course, you don't have to give your book away. Another way of enticing your fans with free stuff is including a short, free excerpt on your site, bring traffic directly to you instead of using a store. You could even give away a whole eBook or a short story, once again it's up to you! Just make sure that you're always harvesting that all-important data.

Competitions

If you're wondering how you can do giveaways of your print books, try the Goodreads giveaway function, which is open to all authors. All you have to do is enter your book's details, set the length of time you want the giveaway to run and how many books you'd like to give away (I'd recommend at least one month and two or three books). Goodreads then posts your competition in their popular giveaways section, which is open to all Goodreads members. It's worked well for me in the past, particularly just before book releases. The only cost to you is shipping the books, so make sure you give that some thought before kicking one off, especially if you're opening up your giveaway to far-flung countries.

You can also run competitions on Facebook or Twitter. For instance, you could pose questions and offer free copies for the first right answer. You could give away signed books or exclusive merch in return for a certain number of shares or likes or sign-ups. Done right, these sorts of promotions can have real impact. It's all about keeping your fans engaged and keeping those plates spinning!

So in summary...

Before we move on to our very final section, let's look back at all the aspects that we've discussed in the **Promote It** section:

● As we heard from our good friend Wikipedia: marketing is the '**process of communicating the value of a product or service to customers, for the purpose of selling that product or service**'.

● Marketing therefore has four primary **goals**:

1. To generate awareness and increase visibility.
2. To convert that awareness into sales by convincing consumers to purchase your book.
3. To forge relationships with customers.
4. To provide data about consumer behaviour so we can market smarter.

● The Shelf Help theory of marketing revolves around **the funnel**. The funnel is a process that first creates fans and then turns them into friends – zealots who will market your books for you. Besides selling books, this should be your number one goal when you're marketing. Why? Because word-of-mouth marketing is the most powerful form of marketing, and friends – or zealots – are the ones who will do it for you. Remember, you aren't the only one who can market your books.

● There are various marketing methods available to today's author, and they can be roughly divided into two camps – **active** and **organic**. Active methods involve input and effort from you, for example boosting posts on Facebook, or organising a signing. Organic methods involve making your book available on plenty of sites and allowing word-of-mouth to happen. Active methods invariably happen at the top of the funnel, resulting in the organic methods taking over at the bottom, feeding right back into the top.

● It's important to remember that not all methods will suit every author, but it's important to **look into everything** at least once, so that you are aware of your options and opportunities.

● Whatever marketing method we use, we should always **gather data** where possible. Data helps us to understand which methods work and which don't. This means we're able to make changes and market smarter.

● The **Five Golden Rules of marketing** are as follows:

1. Always gather data when possible, whatever you do and however you market.
2. Never change two things at the same time as it can muddy your data and analysis.
3. Always keep your goal in mind, whatever it may be, so that you can measure whether you've reached it or not.

4. Never spend a penny on marketing methods unless you're confident you can make it back, either in terms of sales or general awareness.
5. Lastly, try everything at least once!

- A **website** is your primary digital presence on the net, and therefore, *vital*. A website lets you be globally accessible and works around the clock. Where design is concerned, always keep it simple yet interesting. Websites are your personal platform and help you to make friends out of fans. Since it's your website, you're in complete control of the content, design, and functionality. Make sure your site offers everything fans might want and leads them down that funnel.

- **Be social on social media**. Twitter and Facebook don't exist for blasting out impersonal adverts and uninteresting content. They are places where you can engage with readers, fellow authors, and industry pros. They are not sales media – they are for forging relationships and making contacts. Sharing a variety of content on social media is very important indeed, as is being relevant and interesting. Just don't forget that your profile is public and that any reputation is fragile. Be mindful of what you post.

- **Reviews** are very important as they are a form of word-of-mouth marketing, so sourcing them is an important task indeed. Reviews can take the form of stars and scores, written reviews at online stores, reviews on blogs and in publications, and quotes on the cover of your book. It's important to focus on all four types if you can. Review marketing actually starts at the writing phase, as the strength of your story will largely dictate the sort of reviews you'll get. After it's published, you can actively source reviews by making your books easy to share, asking your fans and friends directly, and talking to review blogs and sites. Hopefully this will result in a lot of organic marketing.

- **But reviews aren't the only way of getting your name and your books out there.** Whatever your genre, subject, or area of expertise, there are plenty of websites out there that might be willing to give you some space for an author interview, a guest blog, giveaway or competition. The options are wide and open here and it's a chance to think outside the box. First you have to work out your **USP** – your unique selling point, or in other words, the reason that a site or blog might feature you. It could be a story, some advice, anything. Next you build a list of potential places where your angle can fit, where it's relevant to the readership. Then all you have to do is get emailing!

- **Content marketing** can take many forms and is designed to inspire loyalty in your fans by 'delivering consistent, ongoing valuable information'. This can take the form of short stories, giveaways, blogs, guides... or pretty much anything that takes your fancy! Once again it's a chance to be quirky and different. Content marketing is all about creating something clever, interesting, and very share-able, while making sure it always leads people directly back to you, your website and your books. More shares, more visits, more sales!

- **Physical marketing** is still a viable method of marketing yourself and your books. There are a few options open to you. You could try to get into the local or national press – which will require a contact and an angle, or USP. You can give away or sell merchandise at events and from your site – effectively turning your fans into walking adverts for you. Or, you can use posters and flyers when advertising an event or a new book – spreading the word the good old-fashioned way. Just don't forget to add a little digital flavour to your physical marketing with things like mailing list sign-up forms, QR codes and, once again, putting your URL on everything!

- **Signings** are a great way of selling books and making new fans at the same time. There are two places you can do a signing: at a venue and event you organise yourself, or in a bookshop. The latter is more cost-effective, but it can be difficult for an indie author to get into a bookshop, especially if it's one of a large chain. If you want to get into a bookshop, you first need to make your books available, whether by a distributor or directly from you. You then have to build up a relationship with the bookshop. The first step is to get your books on the shelf. If they sell well and prove a good investment, then the bookshop may have you in for a signing. Make sure you perform well and it's likely you'll be asked back, or recommended to another store. It's a very active method that can result in some great organic opportunities.

- **Events** such as book fairs, conventions and conferences are great places to get your name out there, especially if you're speaking or taking part. The main rule of thumb is that you never know who you're going to meet at these sorts of events, and the sort of opportunities that might arise. Whether you meet journalists, bloggers, industry pros, fellow authors, or readers, there's usually somebody who can help you get your book out there. Give it a try.

- And lastly, **pricing, giveaways and competitions** can all be used to climb the charts as well as keeping your fans and friends interested. Once again, these are all up to you, and are an opportunity for a bit of clever thinking.

My tips for the future

We've discussed a lot of marketing methods in this section, but by no means is it an exhaustive list. As we discussed earlier, marketing is a strange beast. It evolves and grows with you, and you'll find that what suited you one month might not suit you the next. Ideas might pop up here and there, or new platforms or companies might emerge overnight. The true essence of marketing is constant effort and constant testing – pulling levers here and there and monitoring the result. Along the way, you'll abandon some levers and find other, shinier ones. Some of these levers will grow or shrink in size, while others might get easier, or harder, to pull. And all the while you'll be building yourself a powerful platform from which to market, forging your own well-oiled, fast-moving funnel. This is why my tips for the future are simply to keep learning, and keep going.

Standing on the shoulders of giants

Isaac Newton was a wise man. Aside from sitting under apple trees, discovering universal gravitation, writing the three laws of motion, being a physicist, a mathematician, an astronomer, natural philosopher, alchemist and spare time theologian, he also built the world's first practical reflecting telescope and set the bar for science so high that it took 300 years to reach it.

How can one man achieve so much, be such a paragon of achievement, such a general badass?

There's a famous saying by Mr Newton that might explain it, used in a letter to his scientific rival Robert Hooke, in 1676:

'If I have seen a little further it is by standing on the shoulders of giants.'

Even if Newton wasn't the father of this phrase (it's said that twelfth-century theologian and author John of Salisbury may have been the first to use it), it still rings true. Newton took what others had built, examined how they had built it and then did it better. He learnt from the best, and bettered them. A fine strategy indeed. We authors can do the same. No, scratch that. We *should* be doing the same. Every day.

This is why this final section is devoted to hearing from three authors who have enjoyed self-publishing success, to see what top tips we can glean.

'If you don't ask, you don't get.'

I can still remember my parents mumbling this to each other when I was nought but a young whippersnapper, privately rueing the day they had first taught me that phrase.

The phrase rings true for us indie authors – if we don't ask the questions, we don't get the answers. Well, I've gone one step further and gone out to ask the questions for you!

Below you'll find interviews with three very experienced authors and successful self-publishers. I've asked these great authors a whole range of questions, covering the whole spectrum of self-publishing, from writing, through publishing and straight on to marketing. I've based these Q&As on questions that are regularly asked of me by other authors, as well as common questions frequently typed into

Google. By getting the right answers from the right people, I'm aiming to make sure you don't run afoul of any dubious information. (There is a lot of it out there, after all!).

So without any further ado, let's meet **Hugh Howey**, **Polly Courtney** and **Joanna Penn**!

Say hello to Hugh Howey

Hugh Howey is the best-selling author of *Wool* and the 'Molly Fyde' series. Originally from Monroe in Northern Carolina, Hugh worked as a yacht captain, roofer and audio technician before turning to self-publishing.

After publishing *Wool* independently via Amazon's KDP program, Howey then went on to sign a deal with Simon & Schuster in 2012 to distribute *Wool* to book retailers across the US and Canada. The deal allowed Howey to continue to sell the book online exclusively. He notably turned down seven-figure offers in favour of a mid-six figure sum in return for maintaining his eBook rights. Film rights to the series were sold to Twentieth Century Fox, with Lionsgate also keen to get involved.

You can find Hugh, *Wool*, and the 'Molly Fyde' series at www.hughhowey.com

For those of us who might not have heard of you, why don't you tell us a little something about yourself, your books and accomplishments so far?

Hey, thanks for having me. I guess I would describe myself as a vagabond or a dilettante. I dropped out of college after my junior year, sailed around the Bahamas for a while, lucked into a career as a yacht captain, then fell in love and worked a series of odd jobs in order to be closer to home. I spent two years' roofing, a year pulling wire for an electrical company, and then got a job in a bookstore. It was while working as a bookseller that I did most of my writing. I would get up early every morning and write until I had to clock in; I would write on my lunch breaks; and I wrote at night and on weekends.

I had very low expectations of my work, possibly from working in a bookstore and meeting bestselling authors who still had day jobs. It never felt like a viable career, just a passion that I really enjoyed. I published my first book with a small press after a few weeks of querying, but decided to go it on my own with my second book. I self-published a half-dozen novels in various genres until my short story *Wool* took off. I wrote more in this series, and it went on to hit the New York Times bestseller list several times. The work has been picked up in 30 foreign territories, by Ridley Scott for a feature film adaptation, and has sold over a million copies. When I started writing, I told my mom I hoped to sell 5,000 copies in my lifetime, so you could say that I'm a bit overwhelmed by all that's happened in the last two years.

From looking at your website, it's easy to see that you're a prolific author with many books under your belt. Over how long a period were they all written, and how do you now find the time to write with such a busy schedule?

I started writing in 2009, and I try to write two or three works a year. Last year, I wrote five novels. These are typically 50,000 – 60,000 words in length. I doubt I'll have another year quite like that, as I'm traveling more and more these days. I try to write 2,000 words a day. If you can keep this up, you can write a rough draft in a month. I find that the quality of my writing is vastly improved when I write a lot in a short time. It's similar to how reading comprehension is improved if you read a book quickly rather than a few pages a day. I get out of the flow and voice of my work if I try to write just a bit at a time.

It's not uncommon to hear you refer to yourself as a 'hybrid author'. Would you like to explain what that is and why you chose such a deal?

It's a weird term, isn't it? I will admit to being a hybrid author when I'm pressed, but I prefer to just say that I'm self-published. I wear that term like a badge of honour. I think being an independent author is akin to being an indie musician or an indie filmmaker. You have all this artistic freedom and complete ownership of your work. I'd much rather say this than that I'm with such-and-such a label.

Having said that, I have really enjoyed working with the publishers we've partnered with. My agent and I have done a number of deals overseas, where it doesn't make sense for me to try to market my work or translate it, and in the US, we signed a print-only deal with Simon & Schuster. The idea here is that they can get *Wool* into more bookstores than it was appearing in previously. It was also a chance to test the waters of traditional publishing without committing my digital rights, which is what pays my bills.

What methods or providers did you use to self-publish your books?

Quite a few. I use KDP to publish e-books on the Kindle store, as well as Kobo's Writing Life, Nook Press, and the iBookstore. For physical books, I've used Lightning Source and CreateSpace, though I now have all my books with CreateSpace, as I found that I sell far more physical books directly from Amazon than I do through Lightning Source's expanded distribution. These are print-on-demand books, which have been magical for self-published authors. With CreateSpace, there is zero cost to turn your manuscript into a physical book. No more stockpiling boxes in the garage. They handle the printing and distribution for you.

Another major outlet is ACX, where I have all my books available in audio format with professional narrators. It's amazing how well my audiobooks sell. Authors should not overlook this market.

What can we indies do to stand out from the crowd and prove those doubters wrong?

Standing out from the crowd is difficult, no matter how you publish. As a bookseller, I watched excellent titles come through, fantastic books by unknown authors, and they were returned after sitting on the shelf for six months. JK Rowling couldn't gain traction with her anonymously written book, despite a push from her publisher and an excellent critical reception. That says a lot about what authors face.

Retailers have watched their profits slide, and they blame this on digital publishing, which they associate with self-publishing. Nothing could be further from the truth. Physical bookstores are feeling the same pinch from technology that the music shops and video rental stores felt. This is an inevitable shift, and it is one driven by consumer demand. Unlimited selection, cheaper prices, and home delivery are going to trounce brick and mortar. That doesn't mean bookstores will go away, because I believe they have a special place in too many of our hearts (mine included). But they are going to dwindle. And they are going to associate digital sales and online sales with self-publishing to some degree, which means we get the wrath for what was bound to happen.

I don't think we need to prove anyone wrong. We just need to write the books that make us happy. The thrill is that we're able to publish them without asking anyone's permission, and that's the real revolution.

What are your predictions for us indies and our industry?

I think the next great and tumultuous change in the industry will be when big-name authors begin to publish their own works. In fact it's already happening. JK Rowling published her own digital editions, including the formation of her own distribution network. Jim Carrey self-published his children's book because he wanted full control over the content. This happens in films quite a bit, as actors become wealthy enough and powerful enough to produce their own material. Louis CK did this in comedy, and Macklemore and Ryan did the same with their chart-busting music album. Discovery is the hardest bit. Once you have that, self-publishing is a breeze. Plus, you can afford to hire the best team to help you produce your best work. If you think publishers are in a bind right now, wait until this starts happening.

Because of this, one more trend I think we will see is the betterment of publishing contracts. My print-only deal with Simon & Schuster has a limited term of license. In seven years, I get all the print rights back, no matter what. This is the future of publishing contracts, and it will come about because of the competitive outlet self-publishing provides. You see these same limited terms of license overseas with foreign deals, and it only makes sense in the age of books that never go out of print to limit ownership. In five or seven years, the author and publisher can renegotiate. I think this is only fair, and that we'll see more and more of it.

There are a lot of reasons why self-publishing is awesome. Which reason, in your eyes, is the best?

Creative control. Authors can write genre-bending stories for which there is no bookshelf to place them. It doesn't matter. There are enough sub-categories online, that your book can be in several places at once. Related to this is the second-greatest advantage a self-published work maintains, and that is its incredible lifetime. You have decades for a book to take off. Your work never expires or goes out of print. The full effects of this will not be appreciated for many years.

Say hello to Polly Courtney

Polly Courtney is the author of six published novels. She started out as an investment banker and wrote her first book, *Golden Handcuffs*, because she wanted to expose the reality of life in the Square Mile. Having discovered her passion, she went on to write *Poles Apart*, a light-hearted novel based on her Polish migrant friend's experiences in England. Subsequent novels have covered sexism, racism, fame culture and the summer riots and her most recent novel, *Feral Youth*, is all about disenfranchised youth in a summer of discontent. She is a passionate champion of the underdog and this is reflected in her novels as well as her broadcast appearances.

In late 2011, Polly famously walked out on her publisher, HarperCollins, for the 'girly' titles and covers assigned to her books – most notably her book *It's a Man's World*, the hard-hitting take on the lads' mag industry and its impact on society.

Hi Polly, can you tell us about your history as an author?

I didn't originally intend to be a writer. My degree in mechanical engineering led me into a career in investment banking – a career that turned out to be very different to the glamorous one I'd been sold as a naïve undergraduate. It was only when I started sharing anecdotes from my life with friends outside the city that I realised I had a story to tell. I wanted to expose the darker side of this industry that had, until that point, been held in high regard. Back in 2006 however, traditional publishers didn't believe there was a market for such an exposé. I felt differently, and so I self-published *Golden Handcuffs*, just in time for the start of a nationwide obsession with bankers' bonuses and city culture. Before long, *Golden Handcuffs* had made it to the number two spot on Amazon and a literary agent was busy selling the foreign rights in a number of territories. I set to work writing and publishing book number two, *Poles Apart*, based on a Polish migrant friend's story. My self-publishing success piqued the interest of a HarperCollins imprint. I hastily signed on the dotted line, keen to experience life as a 'proper' author. No more muddling along, I thought; no more inventing PR people to field my calls... This was the real deal: the golden ticket I'd been longing for. Or so I thought...

What was it about self-publishing that enticed you away from your publishing house? Or rather, what pushed you away?

My novels have never fitted easily into a genre. They're best described as 'page-turners with a social conscience'. Each one of my novels explores a controversial, topical theme through the actions of a strong, typically female protagonist. Unfortunately, the imprint of HarperCollins to which I had signed was intent on marketing my novels as 'chick lit'. We were at odds from the start, even when discussing topics for future novels. It transpired that my editorial team hadn't read my previous books and just assumed I was happy to fit the mould of their prescribed genre. Each book I wrote with the imprint was assigned a cover that screamed 'girls only!' and frankly, misrepresented the contents. Worse still, each book cover looked entirely different from the last, so 'brand Polly Courtney' was increasingly muddled. Each time I pointed this out, often with the backup of ad-hoc market research, I was told that the decision had already been made and that the package was 'compelling'. I felt as though I was betraying my readers – and attracting a whole raft of new readers who wouldn't necessarily enjoy my books.

Ultimately, what pushed me away was the lack of control I had over the way my books were packaged and promoted. Self-publishing gave me back that control.

How have you gone about publishing your books? What platforms did you use?

For the *Feral Youth* paperback, I opted for a bulk print-run through Troubador Publishing, the same publishing house that handles the distribution. For new editions of my earlier novels, after several batch print-runs over the years, I recently switched to using print-on-demand, again using Troubador for the production and distribution, preferring the print quality and finish to that of Amazon's CreateSpace offering. For ebooks, I do the conversion and uploading myself for Kindle and Kobo, leaving the other channels to Troubador. Amazon is by far my biggest sales platform for both print and ebooks, so having the ability to flex price and update the content in real-time has been invaluable.

Your covers are great! What tips can you give for getting yourself a great book cover?

I have Sinem Erkas to thank for my cover designs. I found her by browsing the shelves of Waterstones, making a note of the designers of covers that felt similar in style to what I envisaged. Sinem was top of my list and available for freelance work. She was even based in south London, near where *Feral Youth* was set. I knew from the moment we met that she'd do a great job. A designer needs to 'get' your book. He or she doesn't necessarily have to have read it, but he/she needs to truly understand what it's saying to the reader. As an author, you should be able to convey this verbally, but it's important that the designer plays back his or her interpretation and that your visions are aligned. If you're not aiming for the same goal at the start, you'll never agree later on. We undertook an iterative process, moving from 'roughs' to a worked-up shortlist and then, with some input from readers and advisors, a preferred design. Social media can be a useful tool for polling fans, if you're willing to offer them a glimpse of what lies under the bonnet.

You're a staunch supporter of the indie ethos. What does it mean to be indie, in your eyes?

Indie publishing is entrepreneurial publishing. It means there is someone – usually the author – in the middle of the operation, controlling all the moving parts. Richard Branson always says he built Virgin by surrounding himself with brilliant people. I believe that's how successful indie authors should think. I certainly don't take on the editing or cover design or distribution myself; I use experts, friends and often readers, too. I like to bring people on the journey with me. If someone offers to help edit my manuscript, they're more likely to spread the word when the book comes out. Indie publishing is all about making things happen – in whatever way works for you.

How do you balance the business of self-publishing with the need to write? Which is more important?

I try to ring-fence my afternoons for writing as that's when I'm most creative. Mornings and evenings are for press interviews, talks, social media, publisher queries, technical issues, video editing and so on. When I write, I ban myself from sites like Twitter and Facebook. As for which is more important... they're inseparable! Neither would exist without the other and I'm fortunate in that I love doing both.

What do you see happening to the indie industry in the next few years?

I believe the proliferation of independently published books will continue and as a result, more efficient filtering and navigation tools for readers will emerge. There will come a time when the vast majority of new titles are published independently, either by individuals or by small author collectives. Traditional publishers will continue to exist, in consolidated form, but only to produce mass market blockbusters by big-name authors. I foresee many of these blockbusters coming from the indie ecosystem, with large publishers minimising their financial risk by taking on titles and authors that have already 'proved themselves'. It pains me to say it, but I have a feeling that the most successful indie writers will be those who are also great self-promoters. Good writing will prosper, but good writing will no longer be enough.

Say hello to Joanna Penn:

Joanna Penn is a person of two halves. By night, she is JF Penn – writer of thriller and crime, author of the best-selling 'ARKANE' series, *One Day In Budapest*, and *Desecration*. By day, Joanna Penn is the author of *Public Speaking for Authors* and *Creatives and Other Introverts*, as well as a professional speaker and entrepreneur. She was also voted one of The Guardian UK Top 100 Creative Professionals in 2013.

Now based in London, Joanna lived in Australia and New Zealand for eleven years. For thirteen years she worked as a business IT consultant for large corporates across the globe, dreaming of writing her own books. After many years thinking about it, Joanna took the plunge, becoming a full-time author-entrepreneur in September 2011.

Hi Joanna, why don't you tell us a little bit about your self-publishing journey so far?

In 2008, before the Kindle, before self-publishing was cool, I self-published my first non-fiction book and made a huge mistake. I printed 2000 books without any way to distribute them or any knowledge of marketing. I was so excited to hold my book in my hands, but then the disappointment set in as I realised that no one would buy them because no one knew I existed. So I learned about PR and made it onto national TV, radio and into the newspapers, but still made only a few sales. So I started learning about online marketing, and began TheCreativePenn.com in December 2008 to share my lessons learned as well as build my own platform.

By the time I published my first novel, *Pentecost*, in 2011, I had built up an audience of people who were interested in reading my book, and the technology, through Amazon KDP and CreateSpace, was available to sell and distribute globally without a massive outlay for printing. I now have four in the 'ARKANE' series of thrillers and my new crime novel, *Desecration*, out now under J.F. Penn as well as a short story series. I continue to write non-fiction under Joanna Penn, including the #1 bestseller *How to Market a Book*. I also continue to share the journey at my website TheCreativePenn.com. It's an amazing time to be an author!

Aside from your writing career as J.F. Penn, you offer a lot of advice and assistance to self-publishers. How difficult is it to manage your time? How do you stay focused on the writing?

I am a scheduling nut! I use a physical Filofax to plan my time, generally months ahead for things like podcast interviews and professional speaking engagements. I also schedule time to go to the London Library and write, as getting out of the house shifts my mind-set. I use OfficeTime on my iPhone as a timesheet, in order to track my hours, because I am committed to spending 50% on creation – writing new projects and putting new things into the world.

The other 50% is on the marketing, admin and business side of things, including social media and networking. I review my hours weekly and adjust if the business side is getting too much. My main focus is always to be creating a body of work in the world, and by my desk is a big sign, 'Have you made art today?' That's my #1 priority.

You're a big fan of the term 'author-entrepreneur' which in this climate is very apt. Why is it important for indies to be a business?

It's only important if you want to do this as a career. If your writing is a hobby, or you just want to put one book in the world, then great, that's absolutely valid. But if you want to make this your living and your life, then you need to consider the business side of things. After all, you wouldn't take a job without knowing how you will be paid, how the contract works and what your working life will look like, would you?

For any business, you need to invest in order to produce a quality product, as well as in your own education. You also need a team around you, so indie authors need editors, cover designers, as well as an accountant to help with the practical side of things. You also need to understand about sales and marketing, not just the craft of writing. I will admit to keeping these two aspects quite separate in my working week. I feel like one of those reversible dolls, where one side is all twinkly, colourful and creative, and the other is in a business suit. But this is my career, my income and my life, as well as my passion, so I think both aspects are critical for what I define as success.

Why is professionalism important to indies?

We're still battling the 'stigma' of self-publishing, and every author that puts out a product that isn't professional gives our critics something to beat us with. Our books should stand next to any traditionally published book and look just as good, and read just as well. In fact, they should be even better, because we are artisans, crafts-people who care about each book and its perfection, not just churning out hundreds a year.

What are your three top tips for marketing a book? What methods can indies use?

Get your book fundamentals right – great book with enticing sample, pro cover design, well-written back blurb/sales description, correct category and keywords (based on research, not guesswork)

Build an email list – put a signup on your site and also ask people to come sign up from the back of your books. When your next book is out, these early buyers will mean your book can chart in a higher position on launch.

Do something/anything to connect with readers and other authors. It might be blogging or twitter, podcasting or Facebook, speaking in person, forums, YouTube. It doesn't matter what, but you need some way to reach people. I can't begin to tell you how much my life has changed because of these online tools – if you're not out there, serendipity can never happen!

There are a lot of predators out there, disreputable companies that can exploit authors. What are your tips for steering clear of them?

Do your research and go buy *Choosing a Self-Publishing Service* by the Alliance of Independent Authors.

Listen to other authors, and get recommendations, rather than listening to companies trying to sell you something. Also, decide on your goals and your definition of success – can this company, or method of publishing, get you to that point?

What are your thoughts on the future of the industry, what can you see happening?

In October 2013, my books sold in 22 countries, including African, South American and Asian markets. It was only a few in each country, but just six months ago, I was only selling in the US, UK, Canada, Australia and NZ.

We've heard that ebook growth is slowing down in the US, but that's not the story anymore. The rest of the world has hardly started in terms of ebook adoption and the next few years are going to be about exploiting our rights in these other markets. I'll be doing some interviews on my podcast, focusing on these new opportunities. I have already started with 'How to publish in Germany' with Matthias Matting and will have another on India soon. It's an incredibly exciting time to be an author, and I see these global markets as the next frontier.

My thanks to Joanna, Polly, and Hugh for their wise words and nuggets of information. That's another great thing about being an indie – you're surrounded by like-minded people, all eager to share their knowledge.

If you have any further questions, then I warmly invite you to email me at the usual email address:

shelfhelp@bengalley.com

I'm always happy to help.

A final thank-you

We may have reached the end of my guide, but it's the start of an exciting journey for you.

I will leave you with a simple, warm thank-you for reading this guide and a few parting tips. I do hope it has been of use to you and I trust my words have carved a smooth path through what might have been a twisting and foreign landscape.

I also want to wish you the very best of luck with your self-publishing adventures. Remember to keep that passion burning at all times – and remember to write, every day if you can. Don't let the business and the admin overtake your primary *raison d'être*, which is to be an author, a writer of books and stories.

Stay professional too. Keep those goals clear and defined. Stay focused and keep your ear to the ground, so that you can be the first to take the inside track. Embrace technology and bend it to your advantage.

Lastly, remember that quality is paramount: in your writing; in your editing; in your cover design; in your formatting and publishing, and in your marketing.

And that's it from me. Go publish some books.

My very best regards,

Ben

Some helpful links

If you'd like to get some more advice then you can find it all at the Shelf Help website. Or, if you'd like to get some advice that relates directly to you and your books, you can also book one-to-one sessions with Ben. Have a look at:

www.shelfhelp.info

In the meantime, please find below a list of helpful links and resources, as well as a handy glossary of self-publishing terminology:

Join today!

The Alliance are a not-for-profit organisation dedicated to supporting indies. If you want to sign up, just scan the ~~QR~~ code to the left!

Authoright

 authoright

Authoright provides professional marketing and publicity services to all different types of authors. Just scan the QR code to find out more.. And don't forget to quote SHELF HELP!

ISBN Agencies

Nielsen (UK)

Bowker (US)

Great blogs for authors

Guardian Books

IndieReader

The Bookseller

GalleyCat

Self-Publishing Advice Blog

The Book Designer

JA Konrath

TheCreativePenn

David Gaughran

The Passive Voice

Website providers

Wix

1&1 MyWebsite

Wordpress

Tumblr

Crowd platforms

CrowdSpring

DesignCrowd

PeoplePerHour

Kickstarter

IndieGoGo

Pubslush

Social media platforms

Twitter

Facebook

Google+

YouTube

Goodreads

Shelfari

LibraryThing

Writing platforms

Wattpad
NaNoWriMo
WritersCafe

Writing tools

Write or Die
Scrivener
Calibre
Adobe Digital Editions

Publishing & marketing providers

Amazon Kindle Direct Publishing
Kobo Writing Life
Barnes & Noble's Nook Press
Libiro
Smashwords
BookBaby
iBooks
Google Play
Lightning Source
Ingram Spark
CreateSpace
Blurb

A handy glossary

A

Acknowledgments: A section of your book dedicated to recognising and honouring the people who may have influenced the book, its publishing, or who might have made a difference to the life of the author.

Advance: The payment that a publisher makes to an author, usually in exchange for the rights to sell and publish their book.

Agent: See Literary Agent.

App: Abbreviation for an application that performs a specific function, such as a reading app, and runs on mobiles and tablets.

Appendix: The part of a book that contains supplemental material, such as tables, references, or extra information. It is usually placed at the end of the book.

ASIN: Amazon's own version of an ISBN, assigned for free when publishing eBooks via the Kindle Direct Publishing platform.

Audiobook: A recording of a book's text being read aloud that can be sold as a separate format in its own right.

B

Backlist: An author or publisher's older and sometimes out-of-print titles.

Back matter: The counterpart of front matter. This means material such as appendices, notes, references, glossaries, bibliographies, or indexes. These are placed at the end of the book. Also called End Matter.

Bar code: Common on almost all retail products – an image made up of lines which encodes a book's ISBN. Normally printed on the back cover of a book. Essential to bookshops when selling or tracking books.

Blurb: The brief description of the book, used for marketing purposes. Can be found on the back of a paperback or on the inside flap of a hardcover. Also a POD provider of high-quality print books.

Binding: The format into which a print book is assembled. Binding types range from case binding, spiral binding, and perfect binding.

Book fair: An exhibition and convention for publishers, authors, or booksellers.

Book proof: A proof is the preliminary, often uncorrected, iteration of a book, intended for a limited audience, such as reviewers. See review copy.

Book trailer: A video advertisement for a book, much the same as a film trailer.

C

Case bound: A type of binding and the industry term for a book in hardback/hardcover format.

Conversion: See Formatting.

Copyright: The exclusive right to make copies, license, and otherwise exploit a literary, musical, or artistic work, whether it be printed, audio, or video. Works are protected for the lifetime of the author or creator, and for a period of 50-70 years (depending on the country) after his or her death.

Copy editor: An editor employed to work on the detail of a book, focussing on accuracy, style and also consistency of formatting, punctuation, and layout.

Colophon: Originally this term referred to the bibliographic information printed at the end of a book, the term is now used almost exclusively for the device or logo of the book's publisher or author.

Cover spread: The entire cover of a physical book, from the front, including the spine, to the back.

D

Dedication: Part of the front matter that dedicates a book to a specific person, place, or thing.

Demy octavo: The name for a very popular book format, which measures 221 x 142 mm.

Developmental editor: An editor who focuses on the overall organisation of a book's content rather than the construction of sentences. A developmental editor is also responsible for re-ordering sections of text, entire chapters, or the re-structuring of a book's plot. The editor may also address the tone, voice, addition or deletion of material, complexity of material and transitions between paragraphs or sections of the book.

Distribution: Making your book available to bookshops and online stores by using wholesalers and distributors.

Distributor: A company that distributes books to retailers, occupying the gap between authors and publishers and the retailer.

Dust jacket: A detachable outer cover that protects the book, printed with the cover design. Usually for hardback/hardcover books.

E

eBook: An electronic version of a book, usually read on dedicated eReading devices such as a Kindle or a Kobo reader, or on devices such as smartphones, tablets, or PCs.

Edition: A specific version of a text.

Endorsement: A written statement promoting an author or their book. Usually placed on the cover or in the front matter of the book.

.ePub: A very popular file format, used mostly by retailers other than Amazon, such as iBooks, Kobo, and Barnes & Noble. Essential file format.

eRetailer: A retailer that sells print books or eBooks via the internet.

Exclusivity: In traditional terminology, this is part of a publishing contract which binds the author solely to one publisher. In the self-publishing industry, it means being exclusive to one particular store or retailer.

F

Formatting: The process of turning a manuscript file (like a Word document) into a format that can be published as an eBook file or printed by the presses of a POD printer. Also called Conversion.

Front list: Traditional terminology meaning books in their first year of publication.

Front matter: Any material that precedes the beginning chapters of the book. This could be the table of contents, the dedication, the acknowledgements, introduction, and foreword.

G

Galley: The interior text of a book after all the editing and formatting has been done.

Genre: A category or style denoted by the content of a book, such as fantasy, romance, or horror.

Ghostwriting: A writer who writes books, articles and stories that are credited to another person. Celebrities often use ghostwriters for autobiographies and magazine articles.

Greyscale: An image with no colour, just shades of black and white.

H

Hard return: Pressing the enter or return key at the end of a line of text instead of allowing the text to naturally move to the next line.

Hardback/Hardcover: A book bound with a rigid cardboard cover, rather than a paper cover.

I

Imprint: An Imprint can refer to the name of a publisher, or a division or subsection of a publishing house that specialises in certain subjects or genres.

Index: Like a table of contents, an index directs readers to specific subject matter in the book.

Interior: The interior content of a book, such as the text and images.

Interior graphics/images: Pictures, diagrams, figures and other items that appear within the interior of a book.

International Standard Book Number (ISBN): A unique 13-digit number (can be 10 or 13 digits if issued prior to 2007) that identifies a specific edition of a book or eBook. UK authors can procure batches of ISBNs from the UK ISBN agency Nielsen. Authors from the US must purchase ISBNs from Bowker, the US equivalent.

J

Jacket: The paper cover wrapped around a hardback.

K

Keyword: An important word or short phrase that can be assigned to a book on platforms such as Kindle Direct Publishing, used by search engines and readers looking for genres, authors, or certain types of books.

Kindle: An eReader produced by Amazon.

Kindle Direct Publishing: A platform provided by Amazon to authors. KDP allows authors to publish eBooks directly to all Amazon stores via a very simple dashboard.

Kobo: A major eBook retailer based in Canada and owned by the Japanese company Rakuten. They have a very wide and profitable global market, and also provide their own range of eReaders.

L

Limited edition: A book printed in limited numbers, usually for special editions.

Line editor: An editor who performs an edit that is heavier than the usual copyedit and that focuses on a book's voice, its tone and phrasing. Fictional line editors focus on the story's pacing, character development, minor details and vocabulary of the period and place where the story is set. They will also focus on the effectiveness of dialogue. A line editor will also focus on correcting the errors in grammar, punctuation and writing style.

List Price: The recommended retail price of a book. Set by the author or publisher and often referred to as the RRP, or recommended retail price.

Literary agent: A person or a company that is responsible for representing authors and their works. Literary agents manage the exploitation of rights in an author's work. They will handle the submission of unpublished manuscripts to traditional publishing houses, negotiate contracts, and also collect monies due.

M

Manuscript: The complete version of an unpublished book before any editing or formatting.

Marketing: The process of communicating the value of a product or service to customers, for the purpose of selling that product or service.

.mobi: Amazon's own eBook format. For reading books on Kindle devices and apps.

N

Nook: A brand of eReader developed by Barnes & Noble.

O

Offset printing: Printing technology where ink is transferred from a roller to a printing surface, and then to a page of a book. Used for large print runs. A more traditional form of printing, compared with modern digital techniques. Often combined with lithography, which is based on the principle of repulsion between oil and water.

P

PDF (Portable Document Format): A popular file format produced by Adobe Systems that is commonly used. All formatting and style is preserved within the file. Although eBooks can and are produced in PDF, the format is not as widely used as .mobi or .ePub formats.

Perfect bound: A type of binding where a glue/adhesive attaches the pages at the spine. Usually with a paper cover, hence the more-common name 'paperback'.

Press release: A statement that is distributed to the media announcing upcoming book launches and events.

Print run: The number of copies printed in a single order.

Print-on-demand (POD): A publishing process in which books are printed to order. This bypasses and therefore removes the cost of warehousing.

Proof: A copy of the book, manuscript, or cover produced so that it can be checked by the publisher or author.

Proofreader: An editor who is employed to read through proofs to check accuracy and formatting.

Publication date: The official date from which a book is available to the public.

Publicist: A person who generates and manages media and public attention for a book through writing press releases, arranging events, book signings, author interviews and book reviews.

R

Returns: Returns are books that either aren't sold or have become damaged, and that are returned to the author or publisher.

Review: A published opinion provided by a professional or amateur book reviewer or reader.

Review copies: Books that are provided to reviewers by the publisher or author, usually ahead of the release. See Book Proof.

Royalty: A percentage of the book's list price that is paid to the author.

RRP: See List Price.

S

Self-publishing: A new form of publishing that bypasses the traditional model of publishing, employing eBook publishing platforms, POD printers, and various other DIY techniques to reach readers and markets directly. Is also known as author-publishing or indie publishing.

Slush pile: The 'pile' of unsolicited manuscripts that are sent to publishers and agents. Often not read.

Spine: The thin section between the back and front covers, usually reserved for the title, author name and publisher/author logo.

Spiral-bound: When wire or plastic is spiralled through holes punched along the binding side of a book.

T

Table of contents: This section appears in a book's front matter. It lists a book's chapters and their page numbers.

Target audience: A specific group of readers or a section of the market at whom the book is aimed.

Territory: Where book rights are concerned, authors and publishers can license and own different rights in different countries or continents. As an indie author, we naturally retain exclusive worldwide rights.

Trade discount: See Wholesale Discount.

Trim size: The dimensions of a print book, specifically the page size.

Typesetting: To arrange the interior of the book in such a way so that it is print-ready. Also referred to as formatting, specifically print formatting.

W

Wholesale discount: The reduced price at which retailers or distributors buy books from authors or publishers.

U

Unit cost: The cost of printing and producing a book.

The Complete Guide to Self-

Publishing

WITHDRAWN

CPSIA information can be obtained at www.ICGtesting.com
Printed in the USA
LVOW07s1627100216

474528LV00008B/769/P

9 780992 787110